SOME GREAT IDEA

Good Neighbourhoods,
Crazy Politics and the
Invention of Toronto

EDWARD KEENAN

Coach House Books, Toronto

Canada Council   Conseil des Arts    ONTARIO ARTS COUNCIL   Canadä
for the Arts   du Canada   CONSEIL DES ARTS DE L'ONTARIO

Published with the generous assistance of the Canada Council for
the Arts and the Ontario Arts Council. Coach House Books also
gratefully acknowledges the support of the Government of Canada
through the Canada Book Fund and the Government of Ontario
through the Ontario Book Publishing Tax Credit.

The opinions expressed in this book do not necessarily reflect
those of Coach House Books.

LIBRARY AND ARCHIVES CANADA CATALOGUING IN PUBLICATION

Keenan, Edward, 1973-
Some great idea : good neighbourhoods, crazy politics and the
invention of Toronto / Edward Keenan.
Issued also in electronic format.
ISBN 978-1-55245-266-0
1. Toronto (Ont.)--Politics and government. 2. City planning--
Ontario--Toronto. 3. Ford, Rob, 1969-. 4. Toronto (Ont.)--
History. I. Title.
FC3097.4.K44 2013   971.3'541   C2012-908119-1

Some Great Idea is available as an ebook: ISBN 978 1 77056 326 1.

'A great city, whose image dwells in the memory of man, is the type of some great idea. Rome represents Conquest; Faith hovers over the towers of Jerusalem; and Athens embodies the pre-eminent quality of the antique world, Art. In modern ages, Commerce has created London; while Manners, in the most comprehensive sense of the word, have long found a supreme capital in the airy and bright-minded city of the Seine.'

– Benjamin Disraeli,
Coningsby, or The New Generation

For Rebecca, without whom my idea of Toronto – and most of my other ideas, too – would be a lot less great.

AN INTRODUCTION:

WHAT DOES TORONTO MEAN?

1

I have this notion that cities are just a collection of stories we
tell ourselves about ourselves. At least in part. In a technical
sense, a city is a location, a geographic area in which a lot of
people live close to each other. And of course a city is also an
administrative division that determines how those people manage
to get along, or don't. A city is the setting for stories, sure,
millions of them, public and private histories, biographies, come-
dies, tragedies, manifestos. But the city is also a character in
those same stories, endowed with a history of its own, personality
attributes, motivations and inner conflicts. The city that exists
as a living body in our imaginations is not a passive set
constructed for its players to act upon, but an active participant
in the events that occur within it – its mean streets and cold-
hearted bureaucracy frustrate our hopes, its creative impulses

and playful attitude entertain us, its generosity of spirit and inner resolve inspire us and offer us opportunities. And ultimately, a city is a story built from all the English 101 elements your teachers told you to expect: the narratives of New York, Paris, Detroit or Calgary each have an increasingly distinct arc – composed of triumphs and defeats, conflicts resolved and conflicts festering – that suggests to us what the city will do next, how we should interact with it, where it will take us and how it will define itself.

I'm writing here about Toronto, an interesting case and a city that's sometimes defined as much by the brevity of its backstory and its hazy character traits as by its pre-eminence among Canadian urban areas or its agreeable nature. It's a Gatsby among municipalities. And I'm writing about a time – the decade and a half following the 1998 creation of the Toronto 'megacity' – in which the stories Toronto tells itself, and the various subplots lived by the people in it, have refused to converge into a coherent narrative. Under mayors Mel Lastman, David Miller and Rob Ford, Toronto appears to have been several places simultaneously, living separate and often contradictory – even irreconcilable – storylines.

2

To give you an idea of the place as it appeared to me in the middle of the time period I'm talking about, here's one Toronto story. After work on June 15, 2005, a few of us from *Eye Weekly* (a now-defunct alt-weekly that morphed into *The Grid*, where I now work) wandered up through the late-afternoon sunshine to the Ultra Supper Club on Queen Street West for a Tourism Toronto campaign launch party. The room was full of black leather and dark wood and the kind of consciously articulated chuckling and business-card trading you see at a board-of-trade luncheon. Everyone was given logoed baseball caps and umbrellas as, onstage, a series of multi-ethnic dancers unveiled a new branding campaign, a couple years and a couple million dollars in the making. 'Toronto: Unlimited' was the slogan, with the letters *TO* rolled into a single character that looked something like a stylized toilet seat.

My friends and I huddled near the bar, draining glasses of complimentary champagne and snatching tiger shrimp from the trays of passing servers. We cracked wise about the campaign. Maybe the logo looked like a spermatozoa? Was 'Unlimited' supposed to sound as stiff and corporate as it did? Or as generic? In retrospect, it wasn't a half-bad campaign, based on neighbourhood profiles that highlighted Toronto's ethnic enclaves, but it was the era of *No Logo* and anything as self-conscious as a branding campaign seemed worthy of disdain. I was already drafting a snarky editorial in my head as our crowd retired to the rooftop patio to discuss current events and watch the sun set. The federal government under Prime Minister Paul Martin was finally going to insist on passing legislation recognizing same-sex marriages, a gift just in time for the massive Toronto Pride festival coming up a week or so later, and one expected to result in thousands of Americans rushing into town to get hitched at city hall. Meanwhile, it looked like Mayor David Miller, at long last, would persuade the province to grant new powers to the city so it could become a grown-up government. We debated the merits of a 'strong mayor' system; Miller didn't want extraordinary executive power, but I thought maybe he should.

Night was falling and the regular crowd of Bay Streeters started trickling into the bar. I wandered up Beverley Street with Matt Blackett, the publisher of the then-fledgling urbanist magazine *Spacing*, to a converted mansion where a literary magazine party was winding down. A couple of editors there had liberated a bottle of wine from the bar and invited us to enjoy it with them across the street. We sat on a picnic table in Grange Park – just a few hundred metres from where I'd taken piano lessons as a kid – and swigged from the bottle. We could see the new Ontario College of Art & Design building from there, Will Alsop's weird and wonderful tabletop structure that looked like a shoebox floating in the air atop massive, brightly coloured crayons. And we could see the work underway on Frank Gehry's addition to the Art Gallery of Ontario, where a new spiral staircase would face out onto the park. I invited Matt and our new friends to a dance party I was holding in a Queen West bar that week – a few pals and I had decided we'd like to be nightclub DJs and had started hosting monthly events that, to our surprise, had suddenly become popular. It turned out the literary magazine editors were already planning to attend, and it also turned out we were out of wine, so we all wandered up to Baldwin Street to meet more friends at an Italian restaurant.

On the patio, I ran into my friend David Balzer, an art critic, and we caught up briefly and shared stories of the dozen or more Fringe Festival plays we were each reviewing that week. Inside, a giant banquet table was surrounded by old and new friends, from *Spacing* and the literary magazine, and we drank more wine and ate spaghetti and I spilled tomato sauce down the front of my white shirt and, in the boozy, giddy haze, gradually lost my capacity for creating memories. Eventually Matt and I walked home, heading up Spadina using our new Toronto Unlimited umbrellas as walking sticks, and plotting the ways in which Matt could take over Toronto politics with *Spacing* as a launching pad. We passed the domed glass structures of Dupont subway station and climbed a hill near the railroad tracks. There, Matt showed me how to shut off the lights illuminating the illegally installed billboards that overlooked the streets. If you knew where to look, all you had to do was flip a switch.

And there was a perfect illustration of the sudden influence we felt we could now exert in the city. We were in our early thirties and had magazines and newspapers that would publish our opinions, and friends in seemingly every bar in the city. We were known personally by the mayor and lobbied by activists. If we wanted to have a dance party, we just booked a bar and brought a crate of CDs. And if we saw something we didn't like – like bright lights on a billboard – we'd just go right up and shut it off. Suddenly we knew where the city's switches were.

We parted ways and I staggered another block to the giant loft apartment I shared with my wife, Rebecca. I'd been married for three years and would become a father less than a year later; after spending my twenties taking odd jobs and moving back and forth from my parents' home in Scarborough, I had now spent a couple years earning a living as a professional writer. Rebecca and

I were close to paying off her student loan, and my own adventures in collection-agency dodging were fading into the past. Gay rights were ascendant, marijuana looked as though it might be legalized, a 'new deal for cities' had just been announced, the mayor was about to be in the pages of *Vanity Fair*. The economy was booming, and new condo towers were beginning to sprout up all over the place. Toronto was growing higher, bigger, stronger. I was writing an essay about all the activity I saw happening among my loose circle of acquaintances, about this Toronto moment, for an anthology called *uTOpia*. A neat parallel was forming between my own personal narrative and that of my friends, and the narrative of the city's development. Both seemed to be on an upward trajectory after the fog of the late 1990s and early 2000s.

At home I smoked a cigarette and tried to read for a few minutes before I climbed into bed. Rebecca came in a few hours before the sun rose, her pockets full of tips from her bartending job. She set the alarm and crawled into bed beside me, and as we lay together a train passed on the tracks just behind our building, and the way it gently rattled the floor of our room was comforting. We nodded off to dream big dreams.

Even though I was inclined to take the piss out of Tourism Toronto, it turned out they had it right. For me and Rebecca and our friends and the Toronto we knew and loved, there were no barriers we could see. Our options and our potential, the number of things we could do, be part of, achieve, the dreams we could dream together, the stories we could create, seemed, in a word, unlimited.

3

That's one story. Here's another, from a year later, and way out in the part of Etobicoke near the airport, a place some of us might think of as drive-through country, where a man was preaching about a more limited vision of Toronto. That man was a second-term city councillor named Rob Ford.

Just a few months earlier, Councillor Ford had stood in council chambers attacking the $1.5 million in grants the City of Toronto had given to AIDS awareness programs. His reasoning? 'If you are not doing needles and you are not gay,' he said, 'you won't get AIDS probably – that's the bottom line.' That was just the hum-along hook to an epic operetta dissecting Toronto's $50 million in grant programs. In addition to the fat-cat AIDS establishment, Ford lambasted the cultural hogs at the city trough: the opera, the symphony, the ballet – 'This is so embarrassing. I just wanted to bring it to the attention of the poor taxpayer who is getting screwed left, right and centre by these grants.' Ford was just getting warmed up when his five minutes of speaking time expired, so he asked for an extension, a courtesy granted routinely in the hot-air-filled council chamber. Not this time. Council shut him up.

Later, Councillor Kyle Rae told *Xtra* magazine that he and his colleagues were fed up with Ford: 'I think [we're] embarrassed that we have a buffoon on council. I think he is fairly ostracized within council. It's almost like we're stuck with him.'

Rae was expressing a sentiment that was widespread among the people I talked to regularly. It seemed as if Ford was always baiting all the other councillors and downtown leftists with his politically incorrect speeches. He called people names: Giorgio Mammoliti was a 'scammer' and a 'snake'; Gloria Lindsay Luby was a 'waste of skin.' He once mused about declaring Toronto a refugee-free zone. He drove his minivan to work on Car Free Day and considered laws banning pesticides and protecting trees to be symptoms of 'communism' and 'dictatorship.' He spent only between $2,000 and $8,000 annually on office expenses, shaming those who approached the $50,000 limit (with special venom reserved for expense-account king Mammoliti). He'd once arrived drunk at a Leafs game, shouting obscenities at those around him. He reportedly asked someone sitting nearby if he wanted his 'little wife' to 'go to Iran and get raped and shot' (and then handed some others his business card). When the press asked about the event immediately afterwards, he denied he'd even been at the game. and when proof emerged that he had been there and had been kicked out by security, he recanted, saying he'd been having a rough time personally and had had too much to drink. Back then, he seemed to be nothing but a clown. A bombastic talk-radio freakshow. A street-corner ranter whose demented howling about the demons lurking in the footnotes of expense budgets punctuated every city council meeting. He was an outcast with no political friends who routinely found himself on the losing side of 44–1 votes.

But back then, I did something very few people did: I took Rob Ford seriously. It was an election year, and Ford was running for re-election as councillor for Ward 2 with virtually no opposition. I wanted to understand how this retrograde ranter, who appeared to all the world (my world, anyway) to be an embarrassment, could have been elected twice and appeared certain to be re-elected again. What did voters in northwestern Etobicoke see in this guy that was invisible to me? I pitched the story to my editor as a personal profile that would 'show everything that was wrong with Toronto city politics.' That part, at least, I got right.

It was about 10:45 a.m. on a hot, periodically rainy July day when Rob Ford picked me up in his minivan. He was wearing a blue suit, his blond hair spiky and slick from the rain. I met him near a place on Golfwood Heights where he'd been dealing with a complaint from a guy whose backyard was being flooded by a city-owned drainage ditch. Almost as soon as we started talking, his phone rang, and he answered as he drove. 'Hello. Yeah. Martin Grove and Humber is not today, buddy. Nope, that's not today. Okay.' He hung up and began speaking to me again.

'You see, what I do, I go from house to house. Some people say it's crazy, but I believe, you know, they're the bosses, they're the taxpayers.' Earlier that day, he'd been at an apartment on Kipling. 'I had an MLS [Municipal Licensing and Standards] person with me, and I said, "Come on, you've got to get these cockroaches." You know, they had these cockroaches everywhere. So what we do is, the MLS officer goes to the landlord, says, you know, "You've got thirty days to fix it, and if not, the city's going to come in and get it done." And then obviously it's going to go on their property taxes.'

Then, he told me, referring to his agenda and reading as he drove, there was a tenant on Bergamot trying to get into a larger apartment for her growing family but worried about the price she was quoted. That Ford might be able to negotiate a $200 discount on rent seemed like a stretch. 'All I can do is advocate on her behalf. That's all I can do. These are the buildings here, see,' he said, gesturing to concrete high-rises as we passed. 'They're old buildings. A lot of tenants have been there pretty much their whole life. A lot of them came from Croatia and this is the first place they stayed. So, you know, a lot of them, English is their second language. Some of them, the kids are okay but the parents and grandparents have language barriers. But they're, you know, they manage, and they're hard-working people. I gotta go to bat for everyone, no matter what their income is. No matter what their race or religion is. I treat everyone the same.'

At another house on View Green, an Indian man answered the door. 'Mr. Rob!' he said. Gesturing to the photo of the man's two-year-old daughter on the wall, Ford said he had a fifteen-month-old of his own at home. We had to wait for the appropriate city staff to deal with the man's complaint – he was upset that buses drove up on the grass adjacent to the bus loop down the street – but Ford insisted on waiting outside. 'I just wanted to let you know we were here,' he said. The man offered an umbrella, but Ford refused.

As we stood outside on the man's lawn, I noticed that Ford bore some resemblance to the late comedian Chris Farley, and that there was something pathetically charming about the sight of him there, soaking wet, red-faced in his wrinkled suit, getting drenched in the name of helping out those who elected him. This, he told me, was his favourite part of the job. 'I love my constituents. They are second only to my family in my heart. What I try to do is relate to the average person. That's all I try to be. I hate the word *politician*. People call me "councillor." I don't like that, I just like to be called Rob. I'm just like anyone else. I always tell the community, "You're the boss. Tell me where you want me to be and I'm there. You say, 'Jump,' I'll say, 'How high?'"'

A short time later, back in his van, we talked some more about children, as I had a ten-week-old son at the time. 'He must be crying every three hours, you know. I don't know how we live through it. It's getting better with Stephanie now, she's sleeping through the night. Now the problem is they can't communicate, they can't tell you what they want. You gotta do a checklist: check the diapers, see if they're fed, the gas ...' I said that while that was true, I was also astonished watching my son start to learn about the world. 'That's the learning experience,' he said. 'Unbelievable. They're so innocent. I'm just so amazed by the whole experience.'

He gave me a bit of background. In high school and at Carleton University in Ottawa, he played football: 'I was a centre, I was the guy who hiked the ball.' His dad, Doug Sr., started the family business, Deco Labels & Tags, and then became a member of Mike Harris's Conservative Party under the 'Common Sense Revolution' banner at Queen's Park in 1995. That may be, he said, where he caught the political bug. 'You know, I always had this itch. I was always a communicator, captain of the football team, on the student council. I've sort of been political all my life, even when I was a little tyke. My dad ran in 1995 and served one term there and I was right into it. Because I saw what Bob Rae did, I worked with Davis when I was a little, little tyke, and then I saw Peterson win. Then I saw Bob Rae get in and I saw how the province went from there – it was just a disaster. And then Harris came in and I guess they looked like they're the evil ones, but he got elected and all I kept hearing was "Promises made, promises kept." You may not have liked it, people may not have liked it, but he had a platform and he said he was going to do it and he did.'

As we talked, he came back again and again to how he felt his obligation was doing what we were doing then – helping out constituents rather than blustering at city hall. 'I always tell my constituents, "Call my office first; I will find the right people."' He returned every call to his office personally, often within hours, and usually would make a trip out to see anyone with a complaint, bringing city staffers with him. As we walked around Etobicoke, he was approached every minute or so by people thanking him for help he'd provided or telling him to stay the course in his penny-pinching. If constituents didn't approach him, he often went to them, offering a business card and telling them to call him if they needed anything. I said it seemed like he never told a constituent that something was not his department.

'That's right. The first rule in my office is: never say no. I'll never say no to anybody. But on the other hand, I never promise anyone. I don't use that word, *promise*. I say, "I'll try my best, I'll come out and see you," and, you know what? Ninety-five per cent of the time people are satisfied. You're giving them the attention they want, you've come out, you've paid a personal visit. I like to come out and see the situation for myself because, especially in this area, there's a language barrier sometimes. There's a huge Indian, Sikh population, a huge European population, a huge Somalian population. It's very, very multicultural; it's probably one of the most diverse wards in the city. I've got a little bit of everyone here. I love my job, that's for sure. Helping out people that don't know where to turn. And I always help give them direction.'

He said this is what all those people who hated him downtown were missing. 'When people look at me down at city hall and they read the papers, I can understand how they think I'm a nutcase. But, you know, once people get to know me, they get a whole different perspective.' Rob Ford may have been a raving lunatic, but he was a raving lunatic who would come to your home and stand in the rain to ensure you'd get your fifteen minutes with the city staffer who could help you. And for anyone not familiar with how to navigate the bureaucracy at city hall, and even for plenty of people who are familiar, that was no small thing.

Later that week, Ford gave me a tour of Deco Labels & Tags, which he'd been running with his brothers since his father's retirement. He demonstrated the machinery that put labels on jars and made stickers and other kinds of signs. He introduced me to his eldest brother, Randy, who runs the Toronto plant, and Randy nodded sternly at me when Rob told him I was a journalist working on a profile. Ford told me about how his brother Doug was expanding the operations into Chicago. I asked if it wasn't difficult running a business while being a city councillor at the same time. 'No, no, no. I'm the CEO but my brothers run the day-to-day operation. I come in here, make sure the numbers are where they are. I'm basically the penny-pincher at Deco. I come in once or twice a week to see what's going on, and on Fridays I'm here to make sure the employees and invoices are paid. But you can't do two things at once; it's impossible.'

In his large office at Deco, Ford told me to go ahead and ask him anything – no topic was off-limits. I ran through a list of his scandalous moments. About that famous drunken outburst at the hockey game, he said he wouldn't even try to defend himself: 'I was wrong. And my biggest mistake was lying about it. I don't know why I lied about it. I'm not even a big drinker.' Why did he call Giorgio Mammoliti a scammer? 'He is a scammer, an outright scammer,' he said, pointing to Mammoliti's bloated expense accounts. He said he only bad-mouthed Gloria Lindsay Luby because of some political fight she'd had with his brother Doug in which she'd accused him of wrongdoing; he regretted the 'waste of skin' remark now.

'I'm slowly but surely mellowing out,' he said, but he noted that his fellow councillors marginalized him. They called him a 'fat fuck,' or otherwise mocked his weight. He was constantly enraged by their abuse of the public purse. 'It just annoys me to see how politicians can get away with what they do. It hurts me. They sit there and laugh and giggle, and they think it's a big joke. If the average person doesn't get a free TTC pass, why should we? Why should we get into the zoo for free? Why should we get into the Ex for free? No one else does. Why? I try to get rid of this stuff, and they just ridicule me. You know, we spend $150,000 on free council food, so at every meeting, behind the council chambers, there's a big spread of cheeses, grapes, cookies, all this stuff. It's like, "Guys, you just ate lunch," and at three o'clock, the whole chamber empties out. They're back there like pigs at a trough, literally. And then I make motions, I try to eliminate it, and they laugh and snicker and say, "You haven't missed many meals." They're just such selfish and greedy individuals. It drives me nuts and I'll tell them that right to their face. But it's one against forty-four, you know. Doug Holyday is really my only buddy down there, my personal support team.'

He had no kind words for most of his fellow conservatives on council. 'They call themselves conservatives until they get down there, and then they just spend, spend, spend. They won't even talk to me in the hall. The so-called right wing – like Karen Stintz and Case Ootes – they vote against my motions to save money. I file a hundred motions every budget – we could save $100 million – but I haven't been able to save anything, because they won't vote with me. Not one red cent.'

Did it bother him to be such a loner? He shrugged. 'I don't want to eat lunch with those guys anyway.' And then he said that there was one councillor, besides Holyday, that he really liked personally. Surprisingly, it was the leader of the federal NDP. 'Jack Layton was the one I respected most,' Ford said. 'He sat next to me when I first got to city hall. He really cared about people, and he was ten times better than all those spendaholics they got down there now. I didn't agree with him on very much, we had different ideas about almost everything, but he gave me some good, honest advice about how to help constituents and work with people. He had manners.'

Ford told me he planned to run for mayor someday. He already had his campaign worked out. 'I'll have a basic, common-sense, easy-to-understand platform,' he began. 'The grass is gonna be cut, the litter's gonna be picked up. When you phone city hall you're going to get an answer; you're not going to get bounced around to ten different departments. There's gonna be people that are gonna be accountable down there. We're gonna run it just like a business.' He said the TTC worked only for people who lived downtown; other than Kipling station, the subway didn't serve his constituents at all. There was no subway route to the airport. For people in the suburbs, he said, the TTC was terrible: 'Realistically, we have to invest in subways. We have to get the feds to come on board to help pay for this.' Lastman and Miller's way of bashing the federal and provincial governments was not going to get them to pony up, he said. And he also felt the TTC needed to be declared an essential service so workers couldn't go on strike and hold the city hostage.

Ford said that if the city contracted out services like garbage collection and streamlined its operations, it could easily run on a budget of $6.5 billion rather than the $8 or $9 billion Miller was spending. And that was before you even got into the big banner projects of Miller's administration. The waterfront redevelopment, for example, that didn't, in his estimation, help anyone. 'They get caught up funding huge projects,' he said, 'and, to me, maybe that helps you if you live down on the lake, but it doesn't help anyone here in Etobicoke. You know, people worry about buses, but they just want a clean and safe area. People hear Rexdale, "Oh, it's terrifying," but it's not a bad area. There are some isolated incidents, a few bad people, you know, which come out of the government housing areas. That's 80 per cent of the problems and the shootings, too. Rexdale has more government housing than any part of the city, you know? It's a real balance that you have to practice, if you want to use that word, to keep everyone happy. But to me, Clean and Beautiful City [Miller's civic cleanup program] is just a farce. It's just a make-work program to create jobs for people. I mean, the city's no cleaner than what it was. The graffiti's just terrible. The weeds. Now they can't use pesticides. I never agreed with that, and the weeds are out of control now.'

As he went on, his litany started to sound like a breathless child's Christmas list: 'We're not going to have any fat, the roads are going to be paved, the transit system's gonna be a well-oiled machine, and it's going to be clean, and it's going to be safe, and we're going to have police and there's going to be a police heli- copter. And I'm going to bring in the Guardian Angels ...'

It was time for us to take some photos, and my photographer had Ford put on a neon yellow baseball cap that was hanging in his office. It had 'Team Ford' written on the front, a keepsake from his father's provincial campaign. We decided to go over to the football field at Don Bosco Catholic Secondary School, a place close to his heart. He coached the football team there, and had bought all the equipment to start the program himself. 'I get criticized a lot, because in September and October, every day from three to five o'clock, I'm on the football field. And it drives people nuts. They're like, "You're leaving council to coach football." And you know what? I do. I do leave council to coach football for two hours a day and I come right back to council. I'm back down there at six o'clock. My constituents know it and they agree 100 per cent. These kids, it's unbelievable where they come from. But they're playing football and they aren't getting into trouble. A lot of them have been in and out of jail, a lot of them are in gangs, but they're athletes. And if you give them an opportunity to play football, then it's phenomenal, they can go to university. I'm very, very strict. If they don't have a 60 average, they don't play. If they miss a class at school that day, they cannot play the following day. If you come late to practice? Don't bother coming. It's discipline, and they love it and the parents love it.'

On the field to take pictures, he was playful. He sat in the stands and spread out his arms, grinning wide and turning his head to the sky. He let out a laugh. 'Wait,' he said, 'people think I'm angry, right? I guess I should give you an angry look.' He laughed again, and then contorted his forehead into a frown.

'Think about all the waste at city hall,' the photographer told him. He snarled.

After we were done, the photographer, who'd sat through most of the interview in his office, gave me a lift home. On the way, she said, 'You're going to be nice to him, aren't you?'

'I'm going to be honest,' I said. 'I don't think it will make people like him much. He won't like it.' She looked distressed.

I told her that scratching at the logic behind his 'common sense,' the childlike charm started to appear childish. He claimed pesticides couldn't be as bad as everyone claims because our parents used them and they're living longer than ever – and, besides, weeds are ugly. That we didn't need a tree-protection bylaw to grow the urban forest because 'we've got thousands of trees.' That incineration couldn't possibly be dangerous since 'they use it in close to 90 per cent of the rest of the world.' His facts were often wrong; his math didn't add up; his arguments often seemed at war with logic. His idea to bring the federal government in to pay for subways was a pipe dream. I said to the photographer that I thought his amiable simple-mindedness could be dangerous when it was applied to setting policy.

'Oh, no,' she said, wincing. 'He's just like a big teddy bear. He's so nice. I like him.'

The truth was I liked him well enough, too. Not as a leader or a politician, but as a human being. Even if he didn't appear to be a deep thinker, he seemed to genuinely care about people, and wanted to help them. He was a man with only two real priorities: saving money and responding quickly and directly to what his constituents asked of him. Those were popular priorities, and his approach to them, especially the latter, I thought, could serve as lessons to his city council colleagues, especially those who wanted to beat him.

But at the time, I had no idea he was going to take over my city, and would come to dominate – not just politically, but personally – Toronto's headlines, and hijack my career as a writer. I didn't foresee that one day in 2011, my six-year-old son, when asked to think of a celebrity as part of a family games night, would smile as we ran through every cartoon character and pop singer we could think of before he announced, 'Nope: Rob Ford!' I didn't imagine then that I'd write whole essays about whether or not Ford had said to a 911 operator, 'You bitches, don't you fucking know, I'm Rob Fucking Ford, mayor of this city,' and whether that was justified given that there was a female television comedian dressed like an amazon warrior – a federal government employee, in fact – trying to interview him in his driveway. Or that the city's media would assemble once a week to watch him weigh himself on a giant scale while his brother cracked fat jokes at his expense. I didn't know that his talking on his cellphone and reading while driving – behaviour I'd personally witnessed – would become city-wide debating points. I certainly never guessed that because of Rob Ford, I'd need to return again and again in my columns to seemingly ultra-local issues like bike lanes on Jarvis Street and trivial bullshit like the price and availability of plastic bags in grocery stores. Or that city council would become a long version of *Groundhog Day* in which the same basic issues were debated every few months, decisions made and unmade and made again as the trench warfare meaninglessly moved the battle lines by inches. I never foresaw renowned Toronto-based urbanist Richard Florida telling international audiences that we had 'the worst mayor in the modern history of cities.' Foreign countries would start thinking of Toronto as the place that rips out brand-new bike lanes. I couldn't tell then that large parts of the city would be gripped by a Ford-inspired fever dream in which growing pains are imagined to be symptoms of an illness, and that the cure involved stamping out those things that are flourishing rather than tending to those that are suffering.

After meeting him, I understood Rob Ford to be a guy who would answer your phone call and visit your house to repair a pothole. But the story of the city he told was very different from the one I experienced. So I wrote my story and stopped paying attention to him until his story of Toronto and mine collided in a huge civic identity crisis. How the story of Toronto moves forward in the wake of that collision is a big, puzzling question. What does Toronto even mean? What kind of city is it? What kind of place do we want it to be? That's *the* big question, isn't it?

4

But maybe that's always been the question. The broad strokes of Toronto's history as a city paint a picture of almost constant ascension over roughly two centuries – from a strategic Great Lakes trading and military post, to a manufacturing and economic hub at the centre of Ontario's economy, to the financial and cultural capital of Canada, to a prominent global metropolis. Toronto is, today, among the safest, most prosperous, most livable and most important cities in the world.

But when you study the history a bit closer, you see the story-line keeps halting and doubling back on itself. The whole thing is a chain of struggles: progress is met with reactionary and counter-reactionary movements at every turn; there's a see-saw fight between those pushing rapid change and those battling for preservation, between a drive to centralize power and the desire to share it among an ever greater number of people. The winning sides in those historic battles don't break down neatly along a left/right-wing spectrum (actually, those terms, as present as they are in the public conversation and sometimes even my own writing, seem barely applicable to most municipal issues). But the victors, those who have defined Toronto thus far, have almost always been on the side of greater democracy and more citizen involvement. They've tried to embrace the complexity and contradictions of the city and harness the energy those qualities create. Toronto's always been propelled forward when it takes its lead from the people rather than from power brokers, when it structures its decisions so that the many voices that make up the city can be included in the conversation, when it allows for differences to coexist rather than be ironed out.

And, most significantly, solutions to problems in Toronto have seldom begun at city hall. They generally arrive there from the streets, from residents and business owners, very often those fed up with the visionary foolishness of the mayor or city council. And those changes, when the fires are finally extinguished, come to be accepted and approved and finally entrenched in the identity of the city. Throughout our history, underdogs constantly win. Toronto's collective story shows not only that you can fight city hall (or Queen's Park, or Ottawa), but that often fighting city hall is the only way to get anything worthwhile done. Like the city itself, it ain't necessarily always pretty. *Messy*, in fact, might be the best word. Toronto's charms have often been described as 'messy urbanism,' but we've equally always worked on the basis of messy democracy. It's frustratingly slow sometimes, and often inelegant and filled with conflict, but for better or for worse, it's been what's worked for us. Messiness is kind of our thing.

But what role does the mayor of Toronto play in that messy story? It's a puzzling question. I maintain that Toronto is not and never has been defined by elites or power brokers or visionary leaders. Yet I'll keep coming back again and again, as I tell the recent story of the city, to the mayor. What exactly does a mayor mean to the city he or she leads? In one sense, obviously, you've got the job description laid out in the City of Toronto Act: the mayor leads the forty-four city councillors in drafting bylaws and overseeing the administration of the city's government, acts as the chief executive officer, and is the official ambassador for the city at ceremonial events. But in the grander scheme of things, the job comes with a different, mostly separate and arguably more important function. The mayor is the personification of the city's character and mood. He or she sets the tone and establishes the content of the civic conversation. He or she serves as the public face a city shows itself and the rest of the world, and acts as the voice of the city in reaction to events. The mayor, elected by the people, represents the city's psyche.

Which isn't to say the mayor always embodies the will of the people. He or she can also be a foil, a goad, even a villain. *Toronto Life* magazine called Ford's mayoralty the 'weirdest ever,' but even in Toronto he has some competition in that category, as Mark Maloney once told the *Toronto Sun*. There was Sam McBride in the 1920s and 1930s who was prone to physically assaulting city councillors. There was George Gurnett in the mid-1800s, who stripped an anti-corruption opponent, beat him, covered him in pine tar and rolled him in chicken feathers. His successor, John Powell, shot and killed a rebel reformer. And there was Allan Lamport, who famously said, 'Toronto is the city of the future and always will be,' and spent the equivalent of over $300,000 in today's dollars secretly entertaining guests at the Royal York Hotel while he was mayor in the 1950s. So they aren't all role models, clearly. But in setting the agenda and being the focal point of the conversation, even a bad mayor can come to represent the problems a city sees in itself, and having those problems crystallized in one person's approach can inspire an articulation of alternatives.

According to the thumbnail sketch that's emerged over the past decade or so, the three mayors Toronto's had since amalgamation serve as points on a triangle that represents the divide in Toronto's politics: Mel Lastman was a huckster frontman for established money and power amid the chaos of the early megacity; David Miller was the mayor of pinko downtowners enjoying growing prosperity as the megacity stabilized, oblivious to the frustrations of their fellow citizens; Ford is the mayor of alienated suburbanites who wanted to exact revenge on the prosperous elites of the city represented by both Miller and Lastman.

The characterization falls apart in the details, as we'll see later. Still, voters' perceptions, simplified and distorted or not, are important, and in the ways the leaders conducted themselves as mayor, there is some truth in the caricatures.

We look back on the Mel Lastman administration and remember bumbling, corruption and civic decay. Even as Lastman arrived in office, Toronto had endured a thorough screwing-over by a provincial government that downloaded the costs of transit and social services onto the city, cancelled its subway expansion plans and forcibly dissolved a two-tiered system of regional government that had become a model for the world to create the forcibly amalgamated new city. This larger city was less cohesive than the old municipalities had been – although in functional terms, Metropolitan Toronto had for a couple generations been a single economic and cultural region (one that now extends well beyond amalgamated Toronto's borders to encompass the almost six million people in what is now called the Greater Toronto Area), the places evolved differently and felt remarkably different. Almost all of the old City of Toronto had developed before the world wars as a compact urban streetscape, with low-rise neighbourhoods of mostly Victorian houses on tree-lined side streets running between crowded commercial strips. The inner suburban municipalities, especially North York, Scarborough and Etobicoke, emerged fully planned during the North American boom of the 1950s and 1960s, and featured winding cul-de-sacs filled with bungalows and ranch houses on sprawling lots, separated commercial areas and industrial parks, and concentrations of concrete high-rise apartment towers along broad, high-speed arterial roads. The suburban areas, more expensive to serve and built as shrines to social isolation – or, if you prefer, privacy – had always had higher taxes and lower levels of service, and they tended through the 1980s to be whiter, more solidly middle-class and more conservative politically. That demographic divide started opening up around the time of amalgamation, though the changes hadn't yet become the stuff of newspaper articles, and the political identities – conservative suburbs and left-leaning downtown – were firmly entrenched.

Amalgamation led to an identity crisis. And into that stepped Mel, an unapologetically brash furniture salesman with hair plugs. In private life, Lastman had made it into *The Guinness Book of Records* for actually selling a refrigerator to an Eskimo, and as the long-serving mayor of North York, he was a braggart for his sleepy suburb and a well-known friend to developers. Backed by most of the establishment conservative boys from the old Metropolitan Toronto backrooms, he won office as the first megacity mayor thanks to a big suburban vote lured by the promise of a tax freeze. Under Lastman, whose two terms lasted from 1998 to 2003, the city's politics became mired in controversy. A computer-leasing scandal that wasted tens of millions of dollars gave way to allegations of outright bribery, and confirmed a widespread impression of back-door access for lobbyists in a corrupt administration. Toronto's post-amalgamation budget-balancing strategy during that time became an annual ritual of begging the province for a bailout. The token efforts at official boosterism were uninspired – a generic Yonge Street festival, for instance, or a summer where fibreglass moose were installed around city streets (an idea stolen wholesale from Chicago).

When the mayor took official action in a crisis, he embarrassed us, calling in the army to clear snow or appearing on international television during the SARS epidemic and claiming not to have heard of the World Health Organization. Lastman's personal life and demeanour were even more bush-league – it was alleged that he'd maintained an entire separate family after an affair filled newspapers, and he worried aloud that he'd be eaten by dancing cannibal tribesman if he visited Africa. Jane Jacobs talked about the decline of the city; playwright Deanne Taylor wrote about a *City for Sale*. It was a disgrace.

The bitter taste Lastman's administration left in the city's mouth led directly to the election of David Miller. The son of a working-class immigrant single mother, Miller became an Ivy League–educated lawyer living in High Park. He spoke the language of urbanism fluently and demonstrated a cosmopolitan worldview and confidence common among the city's economic and cultural elites. When he ran for mayor, he spoke of how the city was populated by 'citizens' rather than 'taxpayers' – the difference being that citizens are participants in shaping their city, while taxpayers are simple consumers of services who wonder if they're getting value for money. Miller was an avatar for the communities in Toronto who've shared in the boom times, who have accrued financial or cultural capital or both, who feel they're part of building something. These groups are increasingly concentrated in the most livable parts of the central city, where Toronto's social and physical infrastructure is strongest and, correspondingly, the rents are highest.

Then there's Rob Ford, a university dropout from Etobicoke who disdains sophisticated thinking altogether. His own thought processes tend toward proud simplification and are almost entirely based on the premise that saving money is the ultimate virtue. He's a man who inherited wealth and a political machine, but who's nonetheless claimed to be an outsider. In his own campaign, he spoke forthrightly of the population as straight-ahead consumers of government. He talked about 'respect for taxpayers' and 'customer service' to the exclusion of almost all other topics, and his bottom-line message was that the consumers of Toronto were being screwed over. His own bumbling, inarticulate, unsophisticated persona came across as authenticity, deeply resonating with voters who felt that the last two slicksters left them out of the city's growing prosperity and excitement.

Between the three, you have a fairly neat – maybe too neat – characterization of Toronto's evolving and now decisively split personality in the years immediately before and after the millennium. Now, clearly they aren't entirely representative – they're all white guys, for one thing, and English is their first language – but in their appeal, and even more in their bearing, they demonstrate various aspects of Toronto's psyche. Lastman masked a teenager-like inferiority complex with empty boastfulness and a wholesale allegiance to money men. Miller projected an assured moral righteousness and a confidence in his own smarts. Ford emanates the blind certainty of the wronged, a belief that the successful are suspect and that halting progress will solve all problems. To put it another way: Lastman blustered through the chaos of the post-amalgamation identity crisis; Miller began projecting a self-confident identity onto the new city; and Ford declined to accept that identity in favour of something scrappier and less ambitious.

This book takes a look at Toronto under these three different mayors and tries to explain how we could so quickly lurch from one extreme to another, and then again to another, and how we might proceed from here. It's the story of a time when Toronto grew both literally and figuratively, adding new residents, businesses, institutions and buildings at an astonishing rate, while displaying a previously uncommon civic swagger as it assumed a larger role as a global city, reinventing itself as it has pretty much constantly done in every previous generation throughout its history.

It's also the story of how this messy, sometimes chaotic, process of growth and transformation has led to a new stratification and segregation of wealth and cultural capital, a rapid process of physical and social isolation that led alienated voters to stand up and insist on being part of – or taking over – the city's political conversation. They did this by electing a reactionary simpleton, a walking outrage machine dead set on rolling back many or most of the initiatives that had seemed, to urbanists anyway, like progress. And yet this in turn inspired its own dramatic response – a conversation among citizens – that might see the city finally able to address its outstanding identity questions and real problems and leap forward again.

And it is also, finally, the story of an idea, a simple idea that's long been at the heart of Toronto and one that's made the city great. It's the story of how that idea still points the way forward to Toronto's next reinvention, its next stage of growth, its next great idea of itself.

I

THE MYTHOLOGY OF TORONTO

1

Here's a Toronto moment: I'm at an off-track betting place above the Brunswick House in the Annex. Once upon a time, Albert's Hall, on the second floor of the Brunny, was a legendary blues bar; Etta James played there, Howlin' Wolf, Muddy Waters. It's still a place where people sing the blues, but there isn't any music; today it's a dumpy teletheatre where you can watch horse races from all over world on banks of television sets and gamble on them using touch-screen terminals while swigging beer from bottles or coffee from foam cups. There's a crowd of regulars, made up of some Jamaican guys, some South Asians, a couple old white guys, lots of Asian guys (yeah, guys – there are hardly any women, although not *none* either), all clutching tickets and staring intently at the dozens of screens and occasionally shouting, 'Come on, four!' or 'Eleven! Eleven! Eleven!'

or, most often, just letting out a loud groan at the results from Belmont or Woodbine or Monticello.

You can smoke on the back patio or, rather, on the black tar of the rooftop of the bar below, and look out over backyards down Brunswick Avenue. So I'm out there, squinting at my losing exactor bets, when one of the other smokers starts to make small talk. He's a man in his sixties with a thick Indian accent. Am I married, he asks. *Oh, yes, good, good.* Do I have kids yet? *Oh, three, very good, they will be the source of greatest joy.* Where am I from? *Here! Excellent, you are very lucky.* He moved here twenty years ago. We agree that in that he is far more typically Torontonian than I am, that in Toronto being from somewhere else is completely normal, expected even. 'Who can say what is Toronto?' he asks. 'No one can tell you. We are all Torontonian, people from all over. You like it? Toronto?'

'I love it,' I say.

'Yes,' he says. 'Yes, me too.' He smiles. 'I think it is the greatest place in the world.'

Toronto: the greatest place in the world. But who can say what Toronto is? Everyone can, I suppose, but everyone will say something different. I've been trying to summon up a picture or an episode or a perfect moment that defines *my* Toronto, but the best I can do is a collage of experiences from a mostly charmed life lived in the city, a tourism-brochure highlight reel that's more autobiography than civics.

My Toronto is the home on Victor Avenue in Riverdale where my father grew up, where we'd listen to Poppa play his giant Wurlitzer organ after dinner. Or hear stories about the time he was questioned in the middle of the night in his pyjamas by detectives – they mistook him for a member of the murderous Boyd Gang who'd escaped again from the Don Jail at the end of the street. Bake sales at St. Ann's Catholic Church on Gerrard Street East filled with cousins and aunts and uncles and generations-old family friends who'd pinch your cheeks and sell you back the toys your mother had donated to the rummage table. Schools separated by religion but not race, where my earliest friends were black and Filipino and Korean and Native Canadian;

where some of us lived in the low-income projects at Don Mount Court or Regent Park and some of us lived in the working-class single-family houses on De Grassi Street or Riverdale Avenue, but all of us lived our real lives in foot-hockey games in the concrete schoolyard.

My Toronto means watching from my bedroom window as the 506 streetcar rumbles by, or riding it with all my hockey equipment on Saturday mornings as an eight-year-old for games at Ted Reeve Arena. Or the view from inside a subway car going over the Prince Edward Viaduct, trying to spot two red cars (for luck) on the Don Valley Parkway below before re-entering the tunnel. Or sleeping on the subway in a school uniform in the morning at age fourteen, after we'd moved to Scarborough, and then sleeping on the subway at night on the way home from parties in university.

My Toronto is in the booze can in the alley behind Yonge Street where a girl showed me her fake tiny tits in the washroom before offering me a line of cocaine. Or a Citizens for Local Democracy rally held in a packed church in 1997 where John Ralston Saul gave a speech opposing municipal amalgamation while the silver-haired Raging Grannies sang protest songs outside. Drinking beer and smoking cigarettes and helping plot an election campaign with Jack Layton at the Only Cafe on the Danforth. Standing on the balcony at the Bamboo on the waterfront, watching newly elected mayor David Miller hoist a broom over his head. The crowded, giddy ferry ride to the islands, the manic street drummers outside the Eaton Centre at Yonge and Dundas, the rich baritone of the carny at the Polar Express at the Canadian National Exhibition asking, 'Do you wanna go faster?' and then flipping the switch on the siren that signals the end of the long, laughing, lazy days of summer.

My Toronto is still so much more than that: wandering the deserted streets amid the office towers on King in the early morning, waiting for the subway to start running; being punched in the face by complete strangers on Danforth, on Kingston Road, on College Street, on Peter Street; climbing on the Henry Moore sculptures in front of the AGO. Wandering down Bay Street toward the Sutton Place hotel on the night I was married, with Rebecca still in her wedding dress and carrying her shoes. Watching my oldest two children being born at Mount Sinai Hospital, where I was born, too, and assisting the midwife in delivering my youngest daughter in our bedroom in the Junction.

In Toronto, I've lived in Riverdale, Scarborough, at Danforth and Coxwell, in the Annex, Harbord Village, Bloorcourt Village, the Junction. In Toronto, I've worked for small business owners from India, the U.S., Sri Lanka, Korea, China, the Caribbean, England and Russia. In Toronto, I've worked at a chemical factory in an industrial park and at a day camp in a low-income housing development; I've cut the grass at a military base and along the sides of the highways in North York and Etobicoke; I've been a shoe salesman and a candy-counter attendant at the mall; I've been a telemarketer and walking courier in the Financial District; I've owned a restaurant on Yonge; and I've worked as a writer surveying the civic panorama. My Toronto contains multitudes. It contains my whole life.

Toronto is the setting for my biography, but as I suggested earlier, it's more importantly also a character in it, as it is for millions of other people. Toronto's the place where all those biographies intersect, where personal narratives become social ones, where all our stories come together in one larger story that contains tragedy and comedy and ecstasy and heartbreak. It is our mythology. And we're still writing it.

2

One of the first articles I wrote when I landed a job at *Eye Weekly* was about an unusual, monthly storytelling salon called Trampoline Hall. It was a lecture series, to be precise, but the people giving lectures were not experts on the subjects they addressed, and the narrative of the night was controlled by a scruffy, besuited host named Misha Glouberman who joked about the process of the event ('This is the pre-show part of the show, in which you talk amongst yourselves in anticipation of the beginning part of the show ...'). The audience question-and-answer period was often the most interesting part of the night. It was a big, alcohol-soaked group conversation that was co-founded and run by the novelist Sheila Heti.

Trampoline Hall became phenomenally popular among the literary crowd quickly after it began in 2001. The air in the smoke-filled backroom of the Cameron House every month was charged with self-aware cleverness and a search for larger meaning. It felt very much at the time like a part of Toronto discovering itself. Something about the way the event deliberately lacked polish, and depended for its worth on how the audience supported or antagonized a speaker, its conscious eclecticism and interactivity, made it feel particularly suited to this city. Glouberman told me it had been planned from the beginning to be more than just a series of events. 'We were creating a scene,' he said. And a particular kind of scene, based on getting people together and interacting; the audience was always part of the show, not merely a witness to it. 'Trampoline Hall is about the city,' Glouberman said.

It was at a Trampoline Hall event at the Gladstone Hotel on Queen Street West in November 2003 that something about Toronto crystallized for me. It was just a few weeks before the municipal election, and then–mayoral candidate David Miller had suddenly taken a lead in the polls, a development that had awoken a wave of enthusiasm among young, downtown creative types. Here on the edge of Parkdale, in a neighbourhood that had become a hive of independent art galleries, in a historic hotel whose restoration had made it one of the trendiest drinking destinations in the city, Miller joined a panel for a discussion of beauty.

Specifically, the topic was 'Beauty and the Aesthetic City,' a theme selected by Heti. Although the event was run in coordination with the Miller campaign, Heti insisted that in keeping with the 'non-expert' mandate of the event, the candidate could not give his stump speech, make reference to his platform or ask for votes. Instead, he sat on a panel with Jane Jacobs (who used an old-fashioned ear trumpet as she fielded questions from the audience), playwright Deanne Taylor and novelist Nino Ricci.

Ricci spoke about his experience of Toronto as the child of immigrant parents from Italy. He said he'd grown up feeling a bit like an outsider in Canada, not a 'real Canadian' like those from more established families, because his familial identity was still tied to the culture of Italy. But when he went to visit Florence, he found he was an outsider there, as well, too Canadian to be a real Italian. But, he said, he found in Florence an astonishingly rigid definition of what it meant to be Italian, and what it meant to be Roman or Sicilian or Florentine. Thousands of years of carefully recorded and preserved history had gone into creating that identity, its customs and architecture and art and literature, its cuisine and politics. 'The mythology of Florence had already been written,' he said. It was an atmosphere he found suffocating. Nothing one could do would have the smallest hope of contributing to or evolving the cultural life of the city or the country; Florentines, like people from many of the most storied cities in Europe and across the world, were engaged in a process of preservation, not creation.

Toronto, by contrast, is a young city in a young country, famously grappling with its identity. It's populated by an ever-swelling collection of first- and second- and third-generation immigrants from other cities and provinces and countries. This is what Ricci found exciting about it. 'Toronto is still deciding what it will be,' he said. 'We're still finding out what it means to be Torontonian. Our mythology has yet to be written.' And in that room, among people who maybe had the feeling they were involved in writing a chapter of the city's emerging mythology, or might one day be characters in it, I realized that a quality of Toronto long thought to be a fault was, in fact, one of its greatest assets. It was echoed in something David Miller said at the event, about how he saw his role as a leader in a city of citizens. 'I think being mayor is not about what I can do for you, but about what we can create together,' he said.

Toronto writer Doug Saunders, author of *Arrival City*, a justly celebrated 2010 book about urban globalization, was asked in an interview to compare London, England, where he was stationed for the *Globe and Mail*, to Toronto. 'There's so much invention happening in London,' he said, 'but there's still an undertone of English culture, like the city doesn't belong to everyone. In

Toronto, it feels like everyone is building the city. The most dramatic parts of London's history are in the past, but in Toronto, the next hundred years will be the city's most exciting.'

This is a big part of the story of Toronto, and it's inscribed right into the streetscape on Queen Street East. Eldon Garnett's *Time: And A Clock* consists partly of an archway that looms over the bridge spanning the Don River, and in eighteen-inch-high stainless steel letters, it spells out, 'This river I step in is not the river I stand in.' (A twist on a sentiment expressed by the Greek philosopher Heraclitus, who said, 'No man ever steps in the same river twice,' but a particularly Toronto twist, for reasons I hope will shortly become clear.) It's part of a meditation on time; the river is constantly moving, the water that's there one moment flows on and is replaced by fresh water from upstream, and the act of stepping in the river alters it further – you are now a feature of the river, the water and whatever animals or other things might be in it behaving differently to accommodate your presence. The river is ever changing, and you participate in that change by wading in and getting wet.

As with the river, so with the city. The GTA has, for a few generations, grown by about a million people per decade – a number of new residents in the past ten years that's equivalent to about a fifth of the total population – and more than half the current residents have come here from somewhere else. One of the more obvious and noteworthy effects of this steady growth through immigration and in-migration is that the city is constantly redefining and reinventing itself.

So getting a handle on exactly what characteristics define a Torontonian or the Torontonian attitude is notoriously difficult. Of course, the country as a whole has a pretty storied history of neurosis over the elusive 'Canadian identity.' (Everyone agrees it's not American, and maybe has something to do with health care. And perhaps Mounties. Beyond that, there's a lot of debate.) While it's not surprising that Canada's largest city displays a bit of the same syndrome, it's not necessarily something you see in other big cities: Calgary's a boastful boomtown defined by swaggering energy-industry cowboys, Vancouver has elevated smug granola-crunching to an art, Montreal tangos on the Main in two languages with a bagel in one hand and a rose in its teeth, while the capitals of the East Coast embody a long-suffering I's-the-B'y earthiness. In all those places, they complain about Toronto, but good luck getting them – or us – to tell you what exactly Toronto's all about.

I don't need to go into all the ways in which our cultural output has reflected this. You're likely already familiar with how you can't wander a block through downtown without strolling onto a Hollywood movie set; Toronto is always dressed up to play someplace else onscreen (New York, Chicago or, in the case of the old *Police Academy* movies, 'unnamed American city'). Or how our best actors and directors and writers and musicians have tended to move to Los Angeles or New York or somewhere else. Or even how the most celebrated authors who live here tend to set their books elsewhere – the group of South Asian immigrant writers once identified by *The Atlantic* as the 'Toronto School' largely write about the places they came from, like India and Sri Lanka.

And by now we're all familiar with the complaints about the shabby, makeshift quality of Toronto's street architecture, the little Victorian and Edwardian houses rubbing up against mostly newish and undistinguished commercial buildings. People call the city ugly, and lacking central landmarks and gathering spaces that define the community – as if our lack of shared history and cultural mythology has been made physical through an architectural absence of heritage and monumental definition. It's an undeniable misconception – go to the Toronto Islands or Nathan Phillips Square or High Park or the Toronto Reference Library or St. Lawrence Market and then tell me how there are no great cultural gathering spaces in the city.

But there is some truth to the hodgepodge image. The central city – the pre-amalgamation City of Toronto – *was*, and is, improvised. Cabbagetown, the Annex, Parkdale, Chinatown, the Junction, the Beaches, Forest Hill, Yorkville: all were developed separately, essentially as suburbs on the edges of what was then Toronto, by people escaping the city in the pre-automobile era. Each compact neighbourhood had its own miniature, self-contained downtown. Toronto grew by absorbing these distinct places into itself and, essentially, becoming what Saunders once called 'a place with no distinct core, no symbolic heart, only an evolving and colliding set of human trajectories.'

We are left with a city not of significant focal points but of layers. Layers of successive building trends and uses, immigrant settlement patterns and neighbourhood characteristics, all constantly shifting as new generations and immigrants build their own stories on top of the ones that came before. Suddenly you can see why Saunders and Richard Florida and journalist Robert Fulford all cite Kensington Market as the essential Toronto neighbourhood, and why it's served as the setting for two CBC television series. The oldest institutional structures (fire halls and churches) sit side by side with hand-built vendor stalls tacked onto row houses; it's a place that's housed (and still houses) Christian, Jewish and Buddhist congregations and whose evolution and character has been defined, redefined and refined by waves of European Jews, Hungarians, Portuguese, Asians, Latin Americans and Caribbean people, each adapting the previous group's footprint to its own. The Market is an aggressively unattractive place, one that's magnetic and appealing because of how the people who inhabit it interact with each other rather than how it looks.

3

Around the time I was in Grade 7, I got a job – or what I considered a job – over the March break volunteering for a charity called the Inner City Angels. They funded various projects for youth that today we'd call 'at risk,' and to raise funds for those projects, every year they'd hold a balloon race at schools across the city. Kids would solicit pledges and then, depending on how much money they'd raised, they'd get to release a number of helium balloons from the schoolyard, balloons that would fill the blue sky with a kaleidoscope of colour as the ever-smaller orbs became dots and finally receded from view. The balloons had return-to-sender tags attached so that whoever found them when they landed could mail them back, to tell the kid who'd released it how far the balloon had travelled. It was intended, I assume now, to symbolically reach out to a great big world beyond the marginalized neighbourhood, and illustrate the distance goodwill can take you. Some kids would get their cards returned from Vancouver or South America. My own cards mostly never came back, although I once received one from the faraway suburb of Mississauga, a half-hour drive to the west.

A few of my classmates and I had the task of cutting the lengths of string that would be attached to those balloons, as well as the blank tags that went with them. As payment, we received streetcar tickets to get to and from the office, as well as a couple bucks every day for lunch. Lunch was maybe the best part, because my pals and I would have an hour to wander around the Eaton Centre, find some nourishingly greasy fast food and then window-shop at Club Monaco and Beaver Canoe.

The office itself also seemed to be the coolest thing. It was in a tiny yellow-brick Victorian house standing next to an equally tiny yellow-brick church, in a discrete courtyard bounded by the glass and steel of the Eaton Centre and a couple of adjoining office towers. The mall had actually been built around the house and its church, a piece of local history cradled by this huge modernist monument to the chain-store, indoor, commercial present. The imposing, recent buildings appeared to be huddling around the older structures as if to protect them from the harsh, dangerous traffic of contemporary life – a calm, secret, historic preserve for these frail remnants of the past. And my friends and I had become insiders in that preserve, volunteer employees in the storybook house tucked away amid the relentless, hustling activity of the city.

Later on I would learn that the temple in that courtyard was the Church of the Holy Trinity, a house of worship that was built in the name of service to the poor (and that today dedicates much energy to serving the homeless), and the house itself was Scadding House, named after the first rector of the church and occupant of the adjoining residence. Henry Scadding, an immigrant from England, was the first student ever enrolled at Upper Canada College, and besides the rectory near the Eaton Centre, his name is memorialized today by Scadding Court Community

Centre at Dundas and Bathurst, and a residence at UCC. His dad's wooden cabin home (unimaginatively named Scadding Cabin) is on display at Exhibition Place as the 'oldest house in Toronto' – it was moved to the CNE grounds from its original location on the Don River in 1879.

Besides his work as an Anglican priest, Scadding was a writer and historian, and his favourite subject was the history of Toronto. In his capacity as one of our earliest historians, he gave us one of our fondest myths: the one about what Toronto means. When I say *myth* here, I mean it both in the sense that it's factually inaccurate and also that it informs our lives and explains how we see ourselves and what we value. A good kind of mythology isn't so much factual as it is true, and that's what Scadding gave us. In his 1884 history, *Toronto: Past and Present*, he ventured that the name of the city came from the Huron word *toronton*, apparently meaning 'place of meetings' – a location for different tribes to gather. This is the origin of the name I was taught in grade school, and the one I would have given if you'd asked me while I was working in Scadding's old house. It's an impression of Toronto, and an interpretation of its name, that's been persistent and widely repeated, despite the clarification from subsequent historians that the name of the city almost certainly comes from the Mohawk word *tkaronto*, meaning, 'where there are trees standing in the water.' The vision of those trees standing in the water, picturesque as it may seem, doesn't say much to us about present-day Toronto. Whereas, even if it is inaccurate as history, the definition of Toronto as a gathering place for various tribes is great as mythology: it's a definition that seems truer with each passing year.

An update of that founding myth can be found in a factoid that many Torontonians thought true around the turn of the millennium: that the United Nations had declared Toronto the most multicultural city in the world. You would hear that honour cited in speeches by at least three Toronto mayors, trumpeted in the city's official publicity materials, in federal and provincial reports, in both local newspapers and the foreign press, including the *New York Times*. Yet, as Ryerson geographer Michael J. Doucet detailed in a 2001 paper, no such declaration had ever been issued. The United Nations compiles no official ranking of the most multicultural places in the world.

But it's easy to see why the myth took hold: Toronto is certainly among the most ethnically diverse places on earth. (In 2004, after the 'most multicultural' claim had been debunked, the United Nations did compile a list of cities with the highest percentage of foreign-born residents; Toronto was second after Miami.) Almost 45 per cent of Toronto's population was born outside Canada and, as of the 2006 census, 47 per cent of the residents were classified as visible minorities. The visible-minority population is diverse within itself. Just over a third of non-white residents are Asian, about the same number are South Asian, roughly one in six are black, with Arabs, Filipinos and Latin Americans, among others, rounding out the list. The 311 phone line run by the city offers service in 180 languages.

So, UN declaration or no, Toronto's still an incredibly multi-cultural place, and fairly harmoniously so, too. It isn't like we're a post-racial Shangri-La – foreign-born professionals still have a ridiculously difficult time getting their credentials recognized, for instance, and plenty of racialized residents, Caribbean blacks in particular, still experience a high degree of poverty, crime and profiling by police, among other things. And in Toronto's city government, only five of the forty-four councillors are from visi-ble-minority populations. But one can note the persistence of such problems and still acknowledge that by global standards, Toronto enjoys racial and ethnic peace. The sort of open opposi-tion and ghettoizing one sees between white and black Americans simply doesn't occur here; the sort of ethnic nationalism that's caused recent wars in Africa and Eastern Europe is non-existent; the degree of otherness that characterizes immigrant populations in Japan, say, or that's led to rioting and violence in France, is unheard of in Toronto. Casual racism, or even ethnic stereotyping, is among the ultimate Toronto taboos, and being from elsewhere is considered to be among the most quintessentially Torontonian qualities one can possess.

A whole line of thinking proudly insists this multicultural identity demonstrates how tolerant and open-minded we are.

The whole phenomenon is too often framed, both by those bragging about our virtues and those pointing out our faults, as a social-justice issue, a reflection (or indictment) of our charitable (or uncharitable) nature, a statement on the moral status of our society. It's a misguided, or at least incomplete, argument. Absolutely and obviously, tolerance and open-mindedness are laudable qualities, and fairness and justice are important reasons to fight prejudice and xenophobia. But, really, evidence of our upstanding character is among the least noteworthy things ethnic diversity contributes to the city.

As a source of civic strength, ethnic diversity, particularly from the new immigrants who comprise about half of Toronto's population, gives the city a set of ideas and perspectives to build on that draws from the knowledge, history and traditions of virtually every culture in the world. Joseph Conrad, who achieved fame writing in his third language, English (and had some working knowledge of six languages altogether), reportedly said he couldn't fathom the limited perspective of a unilingual person – his knowledge of different languages allowed him to think different thoughts, in different ways, leading to greater understanding. As a unilingual anglophone, this makes perfect (and lamentable) sense to me.

Different cultural perspectives let you think differently. I've heard that a number of times in a number of ways from business people in my career as a reporter. For instance, from Hadi Mahabadi, who heads up the innovation headquarters of Xerox Canada in the GTA. Mahabadi was born in Iran and moved to Canada as a young engineer after the 1979 Revolution. 'I was very well-known, and I had offers from Japan, Germany, the Netherlands,' he told me in 2010. 'But I knew Canada was a very multicultural place. I knew the social programs were good, how nice Canadians are.' Mahabadi also knew something about innovation – he's the holder of more than seventy U.S. patents personally, and the staff of eighty-nine researchers he leads at Xerox patents about 140 ideas every year. He told me diversity is a key to innovation. 'Innovation is impacted by many factors,' he said, 'but one of the key factors is diversity of thought. When you have a diverse group of people brainstorming, you come up with more and better ideas.' This isn't just a platitude for him, it's his corporate practice: his research centre employs people from thirty-seven different countries, most of whom were educated in their homelands. After the centre introduced its 'diversity of thought' policy to aggressively seek out differences in background for the team in 2004, it saw a 17 per cent yearly increase in the number of patents it produced.

Take that idea out of the corporate realm and apply it to a city. You can see that the density of different backgrounds in Toronto is likewise a resource available to governments and businesses and allows for more and better ideas to take root, for varied experiences and ways of thinking to shape decisions and progress. Our neighbourhoods, too, are shaped by the blending of those different backgrounds. This is evident in the restaurant options available in Toronto, to cite one obvious example: you can take a culinary trip around the world simply by travelling the TTC lines. Kimchee, beurre blanc, wasabi, tabbouleh and chili are all commonplace. Which creates a richer diet for epicureans here, but also sets the stage for innovation: one of Toronto's most celebrated chefs, Susur Lee (an immigrant from Hong Kong), is renowned for a cuisine that effortlessly merges Asian and European techniques and ingredients to create something new.

In 2008, Ted Corrado, the head chef of c5 restaurant at the Royal Ontario Museum, laid it out, explaining how he blended the traditions he learned at his Italian immigrant mother's knee with the internationalism of the city he was raised in. 'Growing up in Toronto, you can't help but be exposed to all the different cuisines, all the cultures we have here,' he said. 'These are things we take for granted – Chinatown, Little Italy, India Bazaar, Koreatown. There are so many options for us. It's what we know and personally it's what I know, and it's how I relate to food.'

This kind of cultural contribution can seem trivial but has a huge impact on how the city functions and feels. When I worked in restaurants, we were always astounded at the love Torontonians have for sidewalk patios – inevitably there comes a day in February when the sun is shining and customers ask you to set up a patio table for them even though it's so cold you can still see your breath in the air. Many of our main streets are characterized by people sitting out on the sidewalk eating dinner or having a drink. This is hardly unique to Toronto, but it is a thing that immigrants brought here: the waves of Italians who arrived after the Second World War were harassed by police when they set up to drink coffee and chat on the sidewalk in Little Italy and (back then) the Danforth. Over time, al fresco dining culture became not just an accepted quirk, but a defining feature of Toronto's streets.

As we talked, Hadi Mahabadi highlighted another way that recent immigrants contributed to his corporate ambitions. In an increasingly global market, he said, employees with experience from around the world bring valuable insight into differing regional needs and preferences, as well as bringing contacts to their home country and knowledge of how to navigate its culture and institutions. It's true of Xerox's innovation office, and truer still for Toronto's business culture. I have heard similar stories over and over again from entrepreneurs. Jeffrey Min, an immigrant from Korea, founded the grocery store chain Galleria in Toronto using contacts back home to open up a supply chain between his native country and his adopted one. In addition to the grocery stores here, he built an empire on a Korean import business and a customer-service management technology that connects consumers here directly with suppliers in Asia. Another example: Toronto clean-tech nanotechnology company Vive Nano was founded in 2005 by Filipino immigrant Jordan Dinglasan. By the time it opened a second office in Toronto in 2010, two thirds of its staff of eighteen were made up of immigrants. The company employed an 'India strategy,' since the giant South Asian nation was known to be interested in nanotech environmental solutions. They said they pursued that strategy largely by networking in the South Asian community in Toronto, bringing on board Toronto-born, ethnic Indian consultant Hari Venkatacharya to help out. Soon the company had contracts in the subcontinent, the bedrock for a long-term strategy based on international sales.

If the world is now defined by global communication and trade, Toronto has within it detailed knowledge of virtually every other country on the planet, fluency in virtually every language, and direct familial and cultural ties to every corner of the world. Like some kind of civic Kevin Bacon, we are connected to the rest of the globe through personal contact. What we're talking about is a cosmopolitan retooling of – and improvement on – the ancient idea of Empire, one based not on conquest and colonization but on immigration and incorporation. It's the strength of embrace: the sun never sets on the Toronto empire.

One further distinct characteristic of Toronto's demographic makeup – and a huge asset to our self-definition as a 'meeting place' – is that the city is overwhelmingly populated by people who have chosen to live here. Only a quarter of Toronto's adult population was born in Canada to Canadian-born parents, and of those a large number moved here from elsewhere in the country. They say there's no Catholic like a convert. Toronto's a city of converts.

4

I've noted the truth in the long-standing complaint that Toronto seems sometimes to have too little shared history, that there aren't enough stories about this place alive in our memories to give it firm definition. But there are some characters from the story of Toronto's past whose names you still encounter.

Bishop John Strachan ruled early Toronto like it was a family business and has a street and school named after him. Metro Chairman Fred Gardiner gave his name to our most controversial road. Nathan Phillips, our first Jewish mayor, has his name on city hall's front yard. William Peyton Hubbard, who served as the city's first black acting mayor in a bunch of interim appointments during his fourteen consecutive terms as an alderman starting in the 1890s, gets notice every year during Black History Month. Lester B. Pearson was a native son who won the Nobel Peace Prize and served as a beloved prime minister, and so we have an airport named after him. Frederick Banting and Charles Best invented insulin in 1921 at U of T, and there Marshall McLuhan foretold how media technology would create a global village. Around the city, places named after Enoch Turner and

Egerton Ryerson and David and Mary Thomson remind us that someone built this place we live in.

In most cases those names exist only on street signs and buildings, and the stories they point to are rarely part of public conversations. But there are three huge exceptions, three figures whose stories are alive in the debate we continue to have about Toronto today: William Lyon Mackenzie, Toronto's first mayor; Roland Caldwell Harris, the city's World War–era public-works commissioner; and Jane Jacobs, the internationally renowned urban and economics theorist and activist. They haunt us still, invoked regularly as founding figures of Toronto whose proud legacy we've inherited. Their most significant acts and ideas, in fact, laid down the principles on which we govern ourselves today. Together they form a Holy Trinity of Torontoism.

About 90 per cent of the curriculum of my history classes from grades 7 to 9 involved the study of William Lyon Mackenzie, the politician, newspaperman and armed insurrectionist who was our first mayor. The guy's kind of an all-purpose civic hero today: Rob Ford, in his first official speech as mayor the day he was sworn in, said he wanted to emulate Mackenzie; City Councillor Adam Vaughan, the mayor's biggest, most vocal enemy, has a giant portrait of Mackenzie hanging on the wall of his office at city hall. We might not all agree on much in this city, but we agree on the rebel mayor.

Born in Scotland, Mackenzie moved here as a young man in 1824 and founded the *Colonial Advocate*, an agitprop newspaper that railed against the ruling class of Toronto and Upper Canada (as Ontario was known in Ye Olde Pre-Confederation Era). In one of his greatest hits as a journalist, he named and documented the membership and activities of the Family Compact, a small brotherhood of bureaucrats who ran the colonial administration like it was a private club. One list reproduced in former Toronto mayor John Sewell's biography of Mackenzie showed the specific nepotism and corruption of the relatives and friends of the inter-married Boulton, Sherwood and Jarvis families, and their friend Bishop John Strachan, including their government salaries.

Mackenzie's rallying cry was democracy, and he carried the mandate for reform into the provincial legislature, where he repeatedly clashed with the royally appointed cabinet. In 1834, he was elected the first mayor of the newly incorporated City of Toronto under a reform banner, promising to end the cronyism and corruption that had run rampant in a city whose population had just tripled in three years. (Take note: the very first mayor of the city campaigned on a 'throw the bums out' platform.) He cleaned house, but his council refused to raise taxes enough to adequately deal with an inherited debt and the desperate need for new sewers and sidewalks. After a cholera epidemic that killed about 5 per cent of the city's population, he led a council that was politically polarized to the point of paralysis. Rather than standing for re-election, he ran for, and won again, a seat in the provincial assembly.

In 1837, Mackenzie led an armed rebellion, marching south from Montgomery's Tavern near Eglinton along Yonge, that was put down in three days. He was exiled to the United States. A decade or so later, when Canada adopted 'Responsible Government' reforms in line with what Mackenzie had been demanding, he was allowed to return. He won election to the new federal parliament, where he railed in favour of more 'true' democratic reforms, including an end to the Church of England's involvement in government administration, stopping subsidies to monopoly railway corporations and abolishing patronage bodies. By pretty much every account, he was a hard guy to get along with, prone to slandering his allies over minor differences of opinion with the same gleeful abandon with which he libelled his enemies, and in his later years he became an outright crank, advocating the takeover of Canada by the U.S. He died in 1861 and is buried at the Toronto Necropolis, which today is right next to the Riverdale Farm on the west bank of the Don River.

Looked at a certain way, Mackenzie was a failure as a politician and a rebel leader. But his relentless advocacy for democratic principles, in a fledgling city in the budding country that would become Canada, is considered by historians to be among the most influential efforts in our history. John Ralston Saul has made the argument that the roots of Canada's 'Peace, Order and Good Government' constitutional framework are contained in Mackenzie's declaration of rebellion.

That Toronto's first mayor was a rebel and a reformer – that is, that from the very beginning we were a city struggling against the tidy, self-serving plans of the elite – is of tremendous symbolic significance. Mackenzie's legacy didn't just emerge from the wilderness; it rose in direct response to a status quo that was corrupt and abusive, and his primary tool for fighting it – the one that proved more effective in the long run than guns – was to draw attention to that corruption and abuse and to demand better. The principles he championed, of open government, fair dealing and the enfranchisement of immigrants and regular citizens, are principles that have continued to propel Toronto throughout its history. Democracy can always be improved, and there will always be an elite – political, economic, cultural – trying to govern the city as they see fit. And often, just as in the life of Mackenzie, that elite will succeed, momentarily, in pushing past a popular uprising only to see themselves cast as history's villains after the persistent struggle of the people eventually changes the structure of that power. Those changes become the legacy that tomorrow's city inherits.

Roland Caldwell Harris – known far and wide as R. C. – wasn't a politician or a rebel, but an inside man, a bureaucrat and the most effective civil servant in our history. If Old Bill Mackenzie's legacy was a little weak in the provision of public works, our second patron saint dramatically corrected the error.

And that wasn't his only difference from the original Hogtown hero. Unlike the consummate outsider Mackenzie, Harris was born and raised in the corridors of power – or at least near them. A Toronto native, Harris grew up close to the original city hall on King Street, where his mother worked as a cleaner. After he was married and working as a newspaper reporter, he and his wife actually lived in an apartment inside the new city hall at Queen and Bay (the one that is now called Old City Hall, the ornate Romanesque Revival building designed by E. J. Lennox that is used today as a court building). Eventually he was hired by the city and, in 1912, was appointed works commissioner, a position he'd stay in for thirty-three years until he died of a heart attack. Harris was an overweight, cigar-smoking, teetotalling, Church of England–attending member of Toronto's Orange Order establishment, who carried a camera and volume of poetry with him wherever he went.

Living inside city hall gave Harris a pretty good look at what problems were facing the city: back then, the building overlooked Toronto's most notorious slum area, the Ward, which sat where Nathan Phillips Square is today. Residents of the Ward and other impoverished neighbourhoods had no indoor plumbing, and sewage ran through the streets to drain untreated into the lake – the source of the city's drinking water. The lack of sanitation probably claimed the life of Harris's own infant son, Emerson, who died of a water-related infectious disease. This tragedy was a commonplace in the squalid Toronto of the period: the infant mortality rate was a staggering 14 per cent.

As the journalist John Lorinc has written in *Spacing* and the *Globe and Mail* – accounts of Harris's life and works to which I owe my understanding of Harris and from which I am largely paraphrasing here – Toronto had been exploding with growth at the time. In the seven years leading up to Harris's appointment as works commissioner, Toronto's population had swelled by 72 per cent and its surface area had expanded 76 per cent through the assimilation of surrounding suburbs. Much of the city's downtown core had burned to the ground in the Great Fire of 1904, but even the parts of the city untouched by flames had very little infrastructure to serve the booming population. The streets were muddy and clogged with traffic and the lake was a cauldron of infectious disease. When Harris arrived in office, Toronto was suffering water shortages that were the result of the deteriorating pipes running in from the lake.

Harris stepped bravely into the crisis, stick-handling various political administrations to commandeer vast sums of money for his building projects. He seems to have been gifted not only at presenting his vision to the public with beautiful drawings and detailed plans and an easy manner with the press (important at a time when all big public-works projects were approved by referenda), but also at navigating both the structure of the bureaucracy and the social systems of the Masons and Orangemen who held power in the city. It was the age of professional bureaucrats – when lifelong civil servants often wielded more power than the politicians, who faced annual elections – and Harris, as the head of the board of control, was Toronto's most celebrated and skilful pro.

Placed in charge of transit, he disbanded the corrupt private operators who ran the streetcars, formed the Toronto Transit Commission and then oversaw the westward expansion of the transit network. He ordered the demolition of outhouses, modernized the sewage system and then established a network of water reservoirs and filtration plants. By 1920, the infant mortality rate had been cut in half. He paved over 1,100 kilometres of new roads and constructed new high-traffic arteries into what were then the suburbs, installed sidewalks throughout the city and oversaw the erection of most of the city's noteworthy bridges. As Dalhousie architecture professor Steven Manell told Lorinc, 'The significance of Harris a hundred years later is that we're still living fundamentally in the city he imagined.'

So Harris built this city. But if you know his name today, it's probably for two projects in particular – projects whose construction was chronicled in Michael Ondaatje's 1987 novel *In the Skin of a Lion*. (Incidentally, that book may be the essential Toronto novel, finding the soul of the city in a native-born Canadian's quest for identity, which he, in turn, finds in the stories of the immigrant labourers who built Toronto's infrastructure. But Ondaatje's portrayal of Harris is wholly imagined, and not based on any research into the man's personal life. Where Ondaatje portrays him as arrogant and conceited, friends and family told Lorinc in an interview he was self-effacing and idealistic; cordial, warm and elegant.) The first of these projects bears his name, the R. C. Harris Water Treatment Plant on Lake Ontario at Victoria Park Avenue. I'm no expert on water-filtration facilities, but I'm confident in saying this one is likely among the most beautiful in the world; the place is a sanitation palace. Surrounded by parkland, it's an ornate art deco structure outfitted with marble floors and brass fixtures, its limestone walls decorated with bas-relief frescoes illuminated by domed skylights. The whole project was designed in detail by Harris, and built during the Great Depression at a cost of $25 million. The place is still in use, the original pumps still working away, filtering 456 million litres of water per day.

The other storied Harris project is also still in use. The grand truss arches of the Prince Edward Viaduct span 494 metres of the Don Valley, connecting Bloor Street to Danforth Avenue, joining together the east and west halves of the city. The bridge's concrete columns topped by rounded sidewalk observation balconies and its black steel-arch girders visually define the vista of the Don River valley, and support the travel of five lanes of car traffic, two bicycle lanes, sidewalks in each direction and east and westbound subways that run under the road. You hear a lot about that subway tunnel: Harris insisted, over apparently strong opposition, on including the lower-level rail corridor to accommodate a subway line, even though Toronto didn't have a subway system at the time (and wouldn't for another several decades). The fight over that forward-thinking provision was just part of the struggle to get the bridge built: the viaduct's construction was subject to four consecutive referenda (it was defeated in one of those years), and city politicians tried various strategies to steer Harris away from the beautiful steel-arch design in favour of cheaper alternatives. He would not hear of it. In the end, the construction of the bridge opened up the east end of the city to more dense, rapid development, and the inclusion of the subway tunnel saved the TTC millions of dollars when the Bloor-Danforth line finally opened in 1966.

The astonishing thing in considering Harris's life's work is the realization that his legacy is the stuff of the city that now allows Torontonians to travel, and keeps them safe and healthy. He recognized that building waterworks and roadways wasn't a matter of grudging necessity; it was – and is – the material of the city that enables all other great civic endeavours, public and private, large and small. That's how he talked about it, too. 'The city is something into which men pour their souls,' he said in a speech at the time. 'A drain well dug is as glorious as an opera or a picture.' He said the men working in the sewers were working for the glory of Toronto. Fittingly, his signature projects are monuments to the city, every bit as beautiful as they are useful.

Faced with an absolute crisis, he built not just to meet the needs of the city's struggling population, but to prepare for the glorious needs of the still-greater future on the city's distant horizon, stretching the water and road networks out into the emerging corners of the city. He taught us to build infrastructure worthy of a great city, for the city we will be tomorrow rather than the one we were yesterday, and to exalt the functions of the city because they enable the great stories of city life to be written.

Which brings us to the figure whose shadow looms largest today, the one closest to our own time: Jane Jacobs. I know, I know. If you live here, or if you live anywhere in North America and participate in discussions about cities and planning, then you can grow tired of hearing Jacobs' name mentioned. If someone brings up city planning or a subject remotely related, the Ghost of Saint Jane will soon be haunting you. At Toronto city hall, I've heard her name spoken at virtually every meeting I have ever attended, by politicians of every stripe – like George Orwell, she's claimed by both left and right and everyone in between. The libertarian American journal *Reason* and the conservative Manhattan Institute have both argued that she was one of their own, while the liberal *New Republic* hails her as the prototypical lefty thinker. She's mentioned by those in favour of increasing density and by those opposed to it. In Toronto, and now also in New York, there are prizes and pedestrian urban storytelling festivals named after her. Her pure ubiquity can get on your nerves.

But there's really no way around her. If you read her book *The Death and Life of Great American Cities* today, you're reminded of why it's the most influential piece on urban planning ever written. She lays out, in plain language and from close observation, the qualities that make cities the world's engines of economic growth and social cohesion, hubs of innovation and creators of widespread prosperity. The book is read as an urban-planning text and an argument against the folly of central plans drawn up on paper by visionaries, but above all else, *The Death and Life of Great American Cities* is an argument that diversity is the essential quality of the successful city, and the successful neighbourhood and the successful street or block or park. Diversity of building heights and ages and types and uses (hence the mania for 'mixed use' and 'adaptive reuse' development); diversity of industries; diversity of ages, lifestyles, cultures and income levels; diversity of opinions in a room making decisions. Jacobs describes the city as an ecosystem – one of organized complexity – that depends for its health on differences coexisting in a confined space. These sometimes act in concert, sometimes in conflict and sometimes in symbiosis, but always rubbing up against each other to create something more vital, interesting, productive and mutually beneficial than any of the single elements could accomplish on their own.

To make it all work, she argued, cities must operate on human scale. Physically, so that people encounter each other on foot rather than from inside cars, and politically, so that those who live in a place will determine the shape of growth and development through their interactions, not have renewal foisted on them by some master plan. Local democracy, the political expression of diversity, is essential. And you need all these qualities present not just in the city as a whole, but in each neighbourhood, on each street, on every block that's going to be successful – just as a complete sample of your DNA is present in every cell of your body.

Originally from Pennsylvania, Jacobs lived in New York City when she wrote the book that would change the world, and she used her own neighbourhood of Greenwich Village as her primary example of urban vitality. But she moved to Toronto (so her son could escape the Vietnam War draft) in 1968, settling in the Annex, and found a city vividly demonstrating the principles she had articulated. The municipal entity that Jacobs lived in when she arrived and for thirty years thereafter – the pre-amalgamation City of Toronto, which people now sometimes call 'Old Toronto' or just 'downtown' to differentiate it from the suburban former municipalities of York, East York, North York, Scarborough and Etobicoke – had long been called a 'city of neighbourhoods.' It might have lacked grand boulevards or monuments or squares, but it possessed a dense network of diverse neighbourhoods jammed up against each other pretty much across the entire length and breadth of the city. You could pick an east-west corridor in Toronto – Queen or King, Dundas, Bloor, Eglinton or any of the others – and walk its entire length with very few gaps in the vibrancy of the streetscape. Outside the few blocks of the Financial District and the University Avenue government and hospital corridor, there was no one place for anything – no 'shopping district' or 'street where all the bars are.' You could find factories and workplaces and shopping destinations and live music venues and tourist attractions all over the city, and in almost every one of those places there was also a large residential population, rich and poor and those in between living and working side by side. (See, for example, the case of Toronto's wealthiest enclave, Rosedale, which, in the 1960s, shared borders and commercial avenues with hippie central Yorkville and the slums of Cabbagetown.)

Jacobs was a leader of what is probably the most storied reform movement in Toronto's memory – and a perfect illustration of how a movement formed in opposition to bad government can come to define itself in the affirmative, and create new proposals from the rubble of those it has defeated. Before moving to Toronto, Jacobs had become famous not just for her book, but for her organized resistance to the New York City expressway-building schemes of bureaucrat Robert Moses. When she arrived here, she quickly found herself in a similar role – trying to stop the construction of the planned Spadina Expressway, and with it an entire network of expressways that would have criss-crossed Toronto.

The expressways had been in the works for more than twenty years by the time Jacobs arrived; the network had begun with the building of the Don Valley Parkway and the Gardiner Expressway. The planned Spadina Expressway was under construction by 1963, and the city planned to build an additional five such autoroutes, razing parts of Rosedale, Scarborough, Eglinton West and either Keele or Clinton Street in the process.

In 1969, the Spadina Expressway (today's Allen Expressway) extended south from above the 401 to Eglinton Avenue. Plans called for it to proceed down along Spadina through the Annex and terminate in Chinatown. But a number of Annex residents who would have seen their neighbourhood bulldozed by the new road began organizing to stop it. Jacobs formed a group called the Stop Spadina, Save Our City Co-ordinating Committee with University of Toronto professors David Nowlan and Alan Powell, politician John Sewell (who was elected to Toronto city council to oppose the expressway in 1969), architects Colin Vaughan (father of current city councillor Adam Vaughan) and Jack Diamond, artists Michael Snow and Harold Town, and many others. They sent around mimeographed newsletters, circulated petitions and threw parties, neighbourhood by neighbourhood. Communications visionary Marshall McLuhan even made a short film to agitate against the expressway's construction.

The Liberal chair of Metro's regional government, Albert Campbell, and the NDP mayor of Toronto, William Dennison, remained firmly committed to the road-building plan. Dennison said Jacobs and her crew were simply a small band of downtown loudmouths protesting: 'Lots of tracks in the mud but really only a very few rabbits making the marks.' After a legal battle, the Ontario Municipal Board ruled in favour of the city's plan. Unbowed, the protesters, now representing a mass movement of Torontonians, appealed directly to the one person who could overrule the municipal authorities: Progressive Conservative premier Bill Davis. In June 1971, Davis rose in the legislature to declare the expressway dead. 'Cities were built for people and not cars,' he famously said. 'If we were building a transportation system to serve the automobile, the Spadina Expressway would be a good place to start. But if we are building a transportation system to serve people, the Spadina Expressway is a good place to stop.' Indeed, the rest of the highway network was eventually cancelled and, in 1972, the movement that stopped Spadina helped sweep a reform council into office that was led by Progressive Conservative David Crombie, nicknamed 'the Tiny Perfect Mayor.'

But the battle had not been purely about stopping a road. The arguments against the road network led to the articulation of a set of environmentalist, urbanist, neighbourhood-based principles – essentially the principles Jacobs had laid out in her book – that found application in building the city. Furthermore, the opposition effort had created an army of activists, artists, citizens and politicians who had rallied together around those shared principles and were now in a position to put them to work. Roughly the same group of people, acting on the same principles, stopped, for example, the levelling of Kensington Market and Cabbagetown, which were to be replaced by new housing projects on the (disastrous, we now realize) Regent Park model. Development guidelines were sharply rewritten to ensure mixed uses and mixed heights, and to make preservation of existing buildings part of the process. The transit system and its service levels were radically expanded into the suburban areas of Toronto on the principle that cars must not be thought of automatically as the main method of getting around.

Crombie's mayorship led *Harper's* magazine to call Toronto 'the City That Works.' During a decade in which major American cities were abandoned by a middle class decamping to the suburbs, Toronto maintained its vitality. The era is widely, and fondly, remembered as a renaissance in Toronto's development.

4

Now that we've taken a trip down memory lane, let's put some of it together and find the themes that tie this Toronto story together. We've got this founding myth of Toronto as a meeting place, now enhanced by an embrace of multiculturalism. And we've got this holy trinity of civic patron saints who show us how Toronto was built and the principles on which it became the city that works. You can draw a neat, tripartite schematic that encapsulates this:

1 from William Lyon Mackenzie: democracy is the foundational principle of the city, a political condition that allows everything else to function;

2 from R. C. Harris: building and maintaining the infra-structure of the city is the most important function of the municipal government, because it is the stage on which all the city's stories are played;

3 from Jane Jacobs: if numbers one and two create the environment that allows the city to build and express itself, then diversity in all its forms is the essential condition of Toronto, the quality that drives it to thrive and grow.

Democracy, infrastructure and – the greatest of these principles – diversity.

This book takes its title from the first line of British prime minister Benjamin Disraeli's novel *Conigsby*: 'A great city, whose image dwells in the memory of man, is the type of some great idea.' Disraeli wrote that London was formed around the idea of commerce; Paris manners; Jerusalem faith; Rome conquest; and so on. If Toronto is a great city, or in the process of becoming one, its great idea is inscribed on the coat of arms, whose motto reads: 'Diversity Our Strength.'

When the city council of the newly amalgamated City of Toronto officially adopted the motto in 1998, they were referring to the combined power of the seven municipalities that had been joined together. Those amalgamated municipalities were themselves amalgamations, made up of dozens of the unique towns and villages that had combined their strengths in the past.

At the time I write this, when city council and the debate about the mayor's capacities appears rent with divisions between the old City of Toronto and the suburban areas of the new city, the idea that this diversity is a source of strength might seem ironic. But the thinking behind the motto – which means so much more, of course, in practice – is a handy reminder that there's more than one meaning to diversity, and more than one dimension to the term as it applies to Toronto.

Earlier, I spilled a lot of ink on how the ethnic diversity of the city is vitally important, and clearly it is. But the recent usage of the word as a direct synonym for multiculturalism does disservice to the city's slogan, since it's just one of the forms of diversity that has made the city great, as Jane Jacobs taught us. (Jacobs hardly touches on ethnic diversity in her seminal book – though at least a third of the chapters deal directly with diversity.) Richard Florida – celebrated and derided in equal measure as an urban guru, and currently the head of the Martin Prosperity Institute at the University of Toronto – has laid out a theory in which the success of modern cities can be measured in part by how ethnically, but also sexually, diverse they are. Proudly multicultural, Toronto is home to the second-largest (and among the most visible) gay population of any city in North America.

The Harvard-based urban economist Edward Glaeser wrote in a 2012 essay in the *City Journal*, citing Jacobs, that the long-term economic success of a city depends on a diversity of industries within the city. The Martin Prosperity Institute, in a discussion paper, echoes this when it describes the 'depth and sophistication' of Toronto's employment diversity. Manufacturing and retail trade, professional, scientific and technical services, health care, finance and cultural industries, among others, are all significant contributors to the local marketplace.

To use a metaphor that the creative-class–touting Florida might approve of, Toronto is not like a masterpiece of classical music conceived by a genius composer, with defined roles in the intricately plotted symphony to be played by various people. Rather, it's closer to a piece of improv jazz built up and added to by various players to create something less harmonious, maybe more challenging and difficult to appreciate, but more exciting and dynamic. It's a piece of music still being composed and recomposed all the time.

But it has barely begun. We're still inventing Toronto, for the umpteenth time in its history, as a city built by diversity, according to the principles of diversity and as a monument to diversity – and that invention is a collaborative project. Understanding all this makes it easier to interpret the craziness of Toronto's recent politics.

II

THE NEW CITY

1

If you're looking for a villain in the modern story of Toronto, it's probably Michael Deane Harris, the twenty-second premier of Ontario. His legacy is hotly debated. He led what he called the Common Sense Revolution, in which he slashed welfare and social-service rates, while also slashing income taxes, and somehow, in an economy coming out of a deep recession and soaring into the Clinton-era boom (the last hurrah of North American manufacturing), managed to increase the provincial debt by $20 billion. Cranky conservatives loved him, saying he was finally sticking it to the teachers' unions and welfare cheats and giving the people back their money. Leftists loved hating him, organizing epic protest rallies at Queen's Park and around the province.

But for the purposes of Toronto's story, the thing you need to know about the former golf pro from North Bay is that, unpromised and unprompted, he radically altered the structure of our municipal government and school boards. And in Toronto this transformation was not, everyone agreed at the time and has agreed since, for the better. His thorough screwing of Toronto went further than that, actually. Harris cancelled an under-construction subway line being built on Eglinton and drastically reduced a planned Sheppard subway into Scarborough into a stubby, mostly useless, tiny North York boutique line. He down-loaded the cost of transit and social services like welfare and low-income housing onto the city, without transferring any means to pay for them. But the thing the premier accomplished that's most bitterly remembered in Toronto is amalgamation. Harris had never mentioned he wanted to amalgamate the cities of Metropolitan Toronto during his campaign. In fact, he was on the record opposing the idea, and suggesting instead eliminating the umbrella Metro government. However, the political estab-lishment of the old central City of Toronto was hostile to Harris's Conservatives – and its mayor, Barbara Hall, and her government were openly defiant of the Common Sense Revolution – while the suburban municipalities had tended to be friendlier.

This political reality seems to have occasioned a change of heart. In late 1996, Harris sent Bill 103 to amalgamate the cities of Metro straight to first reading (rather than introducing a posi-tion paper first, the usual process for such a change). Another surprise came shortly after: a second bill that would make cities responsible for 50 per cent of welfare costs (instead of the tradi-tional 20 per cent), as well as a shift in how education was paid for and a retooling of the property tax system. In total, the changes were projected to cost Toronto about $1 billion per year.

Harris's government said amalgamation would save tons of money; critics said it would likely increase costs. The critics have been proven right. Most of the services that would provide economies of scale through bundling into a larger organization were already amalgamated: indeed, more than 70 per cent of the expense and authority over municipal issues – including police, transit, sewage, water and ambulances – were handled by the Metro government. Meanwhile, what was lost under Harris's amalgamation was regional identity, local control over issues like zoning and garbage pickup and parks, and political representation – the 106 local councillors that represented pre-amalgamation residents were replaced by forty-four city councillors.

I don't want revisit the ins and outs of the debate. But I do want to recall the reaction from inside what is now Toronto. The mayors of each of the former cities – all of them, including Barbara Hall of Toronto and Mel Lastman of North York – vocally opposed amalgamation. A group called Citizens for Local Democracy was set up by John Sewell, whose weekly meetings in downtown church buildings attracted crowds of over a thousand outraged citizens. A referendum was held across Metro, and more than 75 per cent of voters rejected the amalgamation proposal. People were worried at the time about the effects of amalgamation and, especially, that the administrative changes would put a huge burden on the property tax base. But on those issues, there was room for argument. What really seemed to unite the opposition to amalgamation was that it was being imposed unannounced, without even consulting local governments and residents. But even when the existing mayors and councils did consult, holding the referendum, Harris ignored the result. A board of unelected trustees was put in place to impose amalgamation on the former cities of Metropolitan Toronto. And so it was done.

In the first megacity election for mayor, there were two main candidates: Barbara Hall, who'd served a term as mayor of the former City of Toronto, and Mel Lastman. Hall was well-liked in Toronto, but soft-spoken and pinched in manner and sort of defined as a politically correct consensus builder above all else (she went on to head the Ontario Human Rights Commission). Lastman, a famously brazen huckster, was the preferred candidate of the provincial Conservatives and the business and development establishment – he was friends and allies with long-time politician/lobbyist Paul Godfrey and the cabal of backroom operators Godfrey ran with.

It could be argued that the new city, big and shaky and now even more undefined, needed for its first head honcho a larger-than-life personality. If we were going to spend a few years trying to figure out what this new Toronto meant, then perhaps we could paper over our insecurities with a little of the loudmouthed bravado Lastman specialized in. As well, Hall emerged as the candidate of the neighbourhoods of the old City of Toronto, while Lastman, though he was born in Kensington Market and began his business there, was firmly associated with North York and, by virtue of that, the old Metro suburbs. In Scarborough and North York and Etobicoke, where people felt amalgamation would result in their cities being swallowed up and assimilated by the famous downtown whose name defined the new city, having proud subur-banite Lastman in charge seemed reassuring.

Lastman won, and served two terms, essentially running unopposed in his re-election bid. His administration, however, was disastrous, characterized by bumbling and corruption. Under Lastman, and in the newly amalgamated Toronto, official busi-ness was conducted in a climate of chaos, sleaze and incompe-tence. The period is nicely summarized in the case of the MFP computer-leasing scandal. I won't go into depth here – the inquiry's report, as vivid and tightly plotted as a mystery novel, is available online if you want to revisit the sordid details – but it revealed a culture of widespread cronyism and influence-peddling (and even outright bribery) that implicated both Lastman's chief financial officer and budget chief.

Equally important, and equally disastrous, for the city, was the business that wasn't being done. Like, for starters, collecting adequate revenue. In the face of the thorough shafting Harris's downloading program had inflicted, Lastman galloped into office on a pledge to freeze taxes for three years, a promise he kept. But costs were ballooning, and the city's infrastructure suffered. Not only did Lastman stop building at the necessary pace, his council was letting basic maintenance go by the wayside.

Harris, with the help of the feds, also hobbled the Toronto Transit Commission. No other major city in the world runs a rapid transit system by funding all operating costs locally; most American transit funding comes from federal and state subsidies. In the 1980s, under Prime Minister Brian Mulroney and Ontario premier Bill Davis, the operating costs of the TTC were split evenly between the three levels of government. But in the 1990s, the TTC was forced to get 80 per cent of its revenue from the fare box and the rest from the city property tax pool. As a result, basic maintenance was neglected, service levels were cut – especially on bus lines – and ridership dropped. And forget about expanding the transit network to suit the needs of a region that was becoming more populous and, through urban sprawl, more spread out.

From the 1950s through the 1980s, the TTC had constantly built new subway lines and streetcar routes, and added new bus service. Seventy-five per cent of the capital funding for that expansion came from the provincial government. Under Harris (who literally appointed a car salesman as his transportation minister), a series of planned subway lines, including one on Eglinton, was cancelled, and the provincial contribution to capital costs was reduced to nothing. Lastman's government's response was commensurate; it found no other sources of funding to make up the difference and the TTC was slowly strangled. Other than a short, unhelpful stub of expensive, mostly empty subway tunnel running for a few stops along Sheppard that Harris paid to build as a political favour to Mel Lastman (an 'expansion' that required an $8-per-rider subsidy in its first years of operation), the transit network, in fact, started contracting through service-level cuts.

A similar horror story was emerging in the water and sewer systems, neither of which were adequate for the needs of the city's swelling population. And if the business climate of the city can be considered infrastructure, then that was slowly crumbling, too. Between 1989 and the beginning of the twenty-first century, Toronto somehow lost about 100,000 jobs while the rest of the surrounding GTA *gained* more than 700,000. The explanation, according to several reports, was that Toronto had far higher commercial property tax rates than the other GTA municipalities. (Even as our residential property taxes were by far the lowest in the region and among the lowest in the province.) The 1998 province-wide switch to Current Value Assessment of property taxes exacerbated the situation. These high business tax rates gradually reduced the city's commercial and industrial diversity, hollowing out the range of jobs and services available in neighbourhoods across the city, and nothing was being done at Lastman's city hall to address this.

Many of the social services the city was now required to foot the bill for were 'mandated' by the province; that is, the city had to pay for and deliver them but the provincial government dictated the level of service and the cost, taking considerable budget flexibility out of city council's hands. So every budget season began with a rush to slash costs for services that were not mandated by the province, then concluded with a session of begging Queen's Park to write a one-time bailout cheque to get Toronto through the year so the slashing could continue anew the following budget season.

For all that, Lastman's years as mayor had some bright spots. One of his redeeming qualities – or mitigating qualities, anyway – was that he was a glad-hander by nature and he liked to be liked. He wanted to get along, even with his opponents on the new city council, and so he allowed leftists like future NDP leader Jack Layton and his wife, Olivia Chow, to control portfolios that were important to them. As a result, the skeleton of a network of bike lanes was initiated (part of an ambitious bike plan his council adopted); in homelessness strategy, a shift from shelters to supportive housing began to move forward (if a little too slowly); and a bunch of active citizen advisory committees, including a youth council and a pedestrian committee, were actively involved in shaping some city decisions. A vigilant council was able to mitigate damage even without co-operation from the mayor: as head of the audit committee, Councillor Bas Balkissoon noticed some procurement irregularities and doggedly pursued them, leading to the MFP inquiry; a group of councillors was able to defeat a controversial proposal to bury the city's garbage in the Adams Mine, near Kirkland Lake.

But a lot of the real action was taking place far away from city hall. Despite the crazy politics and government chaos, something was bubbling up from the citizens themselves. They were actively working to improve Toronto, sometimes with the city's co-operation, sometimes without. And they were getting results.

For example, in 2001, an activist named Dave Meslin launched the Toronto Public Space Committee, a group concerned about, among other things, urban streets, pedestrianism and the proliferation of billboards. The TPSC approached its work playfully – Guerrilla Gardening campaigns planted flowers on neglected patches of dirt on city right-of-ways; the Toronto De-fence project offered to remove unsightly chain-link fences from people's properties for free; the Billboard Battalion showed up at dull variance meetings to speak against the installation of new corporate advertising. The group was surprisingly successful – fending off a bylaw that would have banned utility-pole posters in 2002 – and gave birth to *Spacing*, a political conversation leader founded and run by Meslin's friend and colleague Matt Blackett (full disclosure: I've been a columnist for *Spacing* since almost the beginning). *Spacing* has been arguably more influential than the TPSC, providing a lively, popular forum for geeky topics like land-use planning and transit, and it quickly became must-read material both inside and outside of city hall.

Another Lastman-era activist took his fight to the city's waterfront and beyond. Mark Mattson has a life that sounds like the basis for a prime-time television drama: part private investigator, part scientist, part crusading lawyer and part media advocate. In 2001, the handsome, forty-something lawyer began patrolling Lake Ontario at the helm of his private boat, the *Angus Bruce*, looking for leaky sewage pipes and other signs of pollution. He took photographs and water samples from contaminated sites, documented the lab results and presented legal briefs on violations of environmental law to the authorities. If they wouldn't prosecute, he sometimes did, utilizing private-prosecution provisions in the Fisheries Act that allowed him to bring criminal charges against companies and governments that broke the law.

'These city cops are not enforcing environmental law,' Mattson told me aboard the *Angus Bruce* one spring day a few years later, gesturing toward a Toronto Police Service boat a few hundred metres from the mouth of the Don River. Pointing at bottles and hunks of unidentifiable crap floating around us, he said it was easy to tell when you're getting close to the Don. 'Just follow the trail of garbage,' he said. 'The laws protecting that river are just as strong as the laws against welfare fraud, which they do enforce, or the laws against smoking indoors or drinking and driving. We've been told that 80 per cent of fishers are checked for their fishing licences while they're on the water. But this river, which is protected by statute, is for all intents and purposes dead.' And the cops, he pointed out, have no training or policies that would enable them to do anything about it.

That's where Mattson came in. A former criminal lawyer, Mattson was, and is, the Lake Ontario representative of the U.S.-based Waterkeeper Alliance, led by Robert F. Kennedy, Jr. The Waterkeeper Alliance's literature at the time compared its mandate to 'an environmental neighbourhood watch' program. Its members roved the lake and the rivers flowing into it looking for pollution, then used legal and public-awareness tactics to try to enforce water-quality standards. The charitable organization Mattson fronted was one of six Waterkeeper groups in Canada, and the only one responsible for an entire Great Lake. When he joined up with Kennedy's group in 2001, he'd already been pursuing much the same goal for more than four years. In 1996, Mattson had co-founded the Environmental Bureau of Investigation ('They pollute, we prosecute' was its slogan), which won, among other court decisions, a judgment against the City of Kingston over a leaky toxic dump.

A tour of the Toronto harbour with Mattson and Krystyn Tully, the executive director of Lake Ontario Waterkeeper, yielded near-immediate concerns. Five minutes into the trip, Mattson pointed out a concrete block near the Redpath sugar factory that was gushing a white froth into the lake. Tully snapped photos as Mattson remarked that they'd return later to take samples. We viewed the south side of the Leslie Spit as trucks drove in to dump construction waste along the shore, adding to a long shoreline made up almost entirely of broken concrete and bricks.

Heading toward the Humber River, Mattson indicated one of his big projects for that summer. 'Sunnyside Beach is a stolen place,' he said. 'It used to be a hallmark of the Toronto social scene. Then they built the expressway and just cut it off.' Beaches were a major concern for Mattson. Asking cities to ensure Lake Ontario is clean enough to swim in might seem like asking them to take responsibility for the weather, but Mattson pointed out that much of the pollution in the Toronto harbour was caused by old city-owned dumps leaking pollutants into the water and city storm drains' sewage overflowing into the water. Besides, he pointed out, the prosecutor's job is not to find a solution, but to point out the problem and assign guilt. 'If you broke into my house and stole my jewellery, and the cops take you to court,' Tully told me, 'they don't have to explain to the judge how to get you to stop stealing. That's not their responsibility.'

Up the Humber River near Old Mill subway station, we encountered King's Mill Park, a Waterkeeper success story. It was a small, grassy marina where families barbecue and people come to fish. It's also the site of a former dump. In 2001, Mattson found that ammonia and PCBs were leaking into the river in outrageous quantities. He took samples and submitted a brief to the Ministry of the Environment. Eventually, in 2003, the site was cleaned. Good thing, too – two fishermen were casting lines nearby.

Activist energy was hardly restricted to the likes of Mattson or Meslin and Blackett. In fact, the further you got from city hall and the issues that typically motivate protest movements, the more you saw the city's business and cultural communities still thriving. In fact, they seemed to be thriving even more than before. Trampoline Hall was one tiny pebble in an avalanche of cultural activity that was creating excitement in a thousand small and large, and variously interconnected, ways. As Misha Glouberman, the Trampoline Hall host, told me then, 'Cultural history is happening.'

There was the Wavelength music series and the monthly Vazaleen, a queer dance party, which together gave birth to a Toronto music scene that produced acts like Feist, the Constantines, Broken Social Scene, Metric and the Hidden Cameras. Outside the clubs, you could find it in the parks: in the mid-1990s, local residents led by local gadfly and organizer Jutta Mason, took over the neglected, drug-infested Dufferin Grove Park and slowly started transforming it into a community hub, installing pizza ovens, rebuilding the playground and adding a weekly farmers market. As Mason once told *Toronto Star* journalist Catherine Porter, the Friends of Dufferin Grove Park, as the group calls itself, has worked against the bureaucracy of the city, finding loopholes in regulations to allow their volunteer construction and supervision of activities, and persistently doing things for itself – with or without permission – rather than waiting for the city to act on requests.

On a much larger scale, this same impatience with city hall also arose in other sectors across the city. In 2002, management consultant and American immigrant David Pecault launched the Toronto City Summit Alliance, bringing together business and cultural leaders to address Toronto's problems – from integrating immigrants, to cultural and business innovation, to poverty – and help foster its growth. In the following years, more than six thousand people would become involved in the group's projects (it was renamed CivicAction in 2010). The MaRS Discovery district was founded in 2000 as a non-profit corporation to incubate innovative new medical and technological companies by bringing together Toronto's academic, hospital, government and business worlds so that research can be commercialized. Housed in a converted historic building on the edge of hospital row and a stone's throw from Queen's Park at University Avenue and College Street, the organization funnelled tens of millions of dollars into start-up businesses in its first decade.

Meanwhile, other neighbourhoods across the city were being dramatically reimagined and gentrified. In part due to simple zoning changes made in the 1990s, former industrial zones were repurposed as pedestrian-friendly mini-villages replete with new retail, restaurants and condominiums (the Distillery District, Liberty Village). The formerly derelict Gladstone and Drake hotels at the edge of Parkdale were salvaged and transformed into boutique hotels and community hubs that anchored a new nightlife strip. At the same time, the Toronto International Film Festival, Caribana and Toronto's Pride festival had grown into some of the largest and most important annual events of their kind in the world.

To detail all of the notable cultural and civic activity taking place in Toronto in the Lastman years and the period immediately afterward would fill an entire book of its own (in fact, it's already filled several books). The point is that everywhere you looked in Toronto at the time – everywhere outside of city hall, that is – it seemed that good things were happening. Cultural history was being made.

Actually, that was true everywhere *I* looked. But in other parts of the new city, a much different story was unfolding.

2

The reports that would demonstrate this different suburban story were still a few years away, but when Lastman was mayor, the new, post-amalgamated city was sorting itself in a fascinating – and not very healthy – way. Or rather, it had been quietly, subtly sorting itself for some time, and the effect of this became statistically significant by the time Lastman was elected megamayor. The suburbs were becoming poorer, much poorer than the old City of Toronto. And simultaneously, the old downtown city was becoming whiter, and the suburbs were filling up with new immigrants and visible minorities.

A report issued later by U of T social-work professor David Hulchanski, *The Three Cities Within Toronto*, compared census data from the years 1970 to 2000 – the latter being the precise midpoint of the Lastman administration – and sounded the alarm at what he found. I will explore the situation of the suburbs in greater detail a little later, but I want to outline the key observations in the report that would impact the city's politics over the coming years.

> 1 Traditionally, most of Metropolitan Toronto's old neighbourhoods, 66 per cent of them, had been middle-income (or mixed-income) neighbourhoods, in which the average salary was within 20 per cent of the average for the region. But over the course of three decades, and increasingly in the decade leading up to 2000, fewer and fewer neighbourhoods were middle-income – there was a dramatic

increase in the number of both high-income and low-income neighbourhoods. By 2000, only about 30 per cent of neighbourhoods were classified as middle-income.

2 In the 1970s, the inner suburbs were the most solidly middle-income parts of the city. There were a few high-income neighbourhoods clustered near Yonge in North York and a very few – seven out of hundreds, to be precise – low-income neighbourhoods in the suburban municipalities. But by and large, York, North York, East York, Scarborough and Etobicoke were solidly middle-class. In 1970, not a single census tract in the inner suburbs was classified as impoverished (or 'very low-income'). By 2000, the vast majority of Scarborough and York were classified as either low-income or very low-income, as was virtually all of the northern half of Etobicoke.

3 Pretty much the exact reverse was true in the old City of Toronto. In 1970, virtually all of the old city south of Bloor Street (and south of Eglinton in the west end) was low-income or very low-income, with high-income neighbourhoods clustered around the Yonge and University subway lines in the north end of the city. There were far fewer middle-income neighbourhoods downtown than in the inner suburbs in 1970, and most of them were clustered at the eastern and western borders. But by 2000, much of the old Toronto was high-income or very high-income. In the east end, south of the Danforth, formerly impoverished neighbourhoods were now middle-income, with a distinctly upward trend line. Outside of large subsidized housing projects such as Alexandra Park, Regent Park and St. Jamestown, virtually all of the old City of Toronto was becoming richer.

4 There was a dramatic ethnic element to this sorting: by 2000, in high-income neighbourhoods, 84 per cent of the population was white. In low-income neighbourhoods, 60 per cent was made up of visible minorities. And the same was true of immigration: in the richer city areas, only 32 per cent of the population was born

outside Canada, while in the poorer ones, 62 per cent were immigrants.

For reasons that Jane Jacobs laid out, the separation of neighbourhoods by income and ethnic status can be a problem for the city all unto itself, since diversity is part of what makes neighbourhoods and, by extension, cities work. But the way this sorting was going down in newly amalgamated Toronto made it even more of a potential, pernicious problem. Unlike the old City of Toronto, the inner suburbs had not evolved over generations to serve different kinds of populations. They were mostly built rapidly and according to the assumption that they would serve a middle-class, car-driving population. Whereas in the old city, where immigrants had traditionally landed and there was always a large low-income population, there were a lot of community and social services available throughout those neighbourhoods. And since these neighbourhoods evolved before car travel became the main way of getting around, most people in the old city could find these amenities and supports – parks, welfare offices, public pools, libraries (not to mention things as prosaic as grocery stores) – within a short walk of their homes. In the inner suburbs, on the other hand, there were very few social-service agency locations, and parks and swimming pools and libraries – just like the businesses located in malls – were designed as regional attractions to be driven to.

But the discontent of the suburbs was still simmering in the background. In the spotlight, the voices creating energy in the central city were ready to take their act to city hall. Like Mark Mattson, who, as Waterkeeper, would host a fundraiser with U.S. Waterkeeper leader Robert Kennedy in support of mayoral candidate David Miller.

3

It's easy to forget now that the election of David Miller as mayor seemed like a revolution at the time – an underdog story of a citizen movement rejecting the officially approved choices presented to them by the municipal establishment.

When Miller announced he was running for mayor in early 2003, my news editor at *Eye Weekly* told me he was the best candidate but that it was too bad he had almost no chance of winning. He was polling at only 8 per cent popular support, behind candidates like scandal-plagued Lastman budget chief Tom Jakobek, conservative business titan John Tory and ex-mayor Barbara Hall. While Jane Jacobs had endorsed him, he had, at the time, the support of only one other city councillor. Miller was advised not to run by many of his own closest allies, who feared that if his campaign managed to get any traction at all, he would split the centre-left vote with Hall and allow Tory to win. By almost every informed observer, the contest was considered a two-horse race between Tory and Hall, and the latter was a prohibitive favourite.

But, facing a dour civic mood, Miller told a clear, optimistic story about where the city should be going. He used the planned island airport expansion in the downtown waterfront as a symbol of neighbourhood-destroying backroom deals that would harm the environment. He adopted a broom as his symbol, and the broom would, naturally, sweep the city clean. He talked about a 'clean waterfront' as a pillar representing environmental sustainability, 'clean streets' as a point about beauty and neighbourhood vitality, and 'clean politics' as a vehicle for citizen engagement and an end to backroom influence peddling. On that foundation, he asked people to imagine a 'magnificent city.' He was pitched in advertisements as a man who looked and thought like a visionary but talked 'like a neighbour.' The key message of his campaign, in a particularly depressing political period, was that the city deserved a better government, and that the citizens would be welcomed into his administration to help build something better, something that more reflected their hopes and dreams, and that would improve the quality of their lives.

By October, Miller had gained the lead, and Hall's directionless campaign saw its support collapse almost completely. It was a race now between Tory's talk of efficiency and ruthlessness and Miller's hopeful message of a clean sweep led by citizens. Miller won narrowly, by 36,196 votes, and to his supporters it looked like a revolution that would transform everything. I mentioned earlier the Trampoline Hall event where Miller spoke eloquently about aesthetics and beauty and the power of citizens. The only other points you might need to know about that night was that there was a crowd lined up in the rain outside the windows hoping they might eventually get in, and that a woman actually got up and cried, saying this was the night she finally fell in love with Toronto.

When Miller sat down with the editorial board of *Eye Weekly*, he swept us off our feet. He said he thought allowing bands to put up posters for concerts was a free-speech issue; that people should be thought of as pedestrians first, cyclists second, transit users third and car drivers last; that the neighbourhood was the most important thing to think about when you think about the city; that environmentalism was a priority. And he spoke at length of cleaning up municipal ethics: 'I think we've all seen that city hall over the last few years has become a place where if you're an insider or a crony, you get your needs met; if you're a citizen, a resident of a neighbourhood, you don't.' He wanted an ethics commissioner, audits of city processes and a lobbyist registry. But he also said leadership style would be essential. 'Right now, the culture basically is, "What the hell does the mayor want? We're going to go run around and say that that's our opinion, even if it isn't." That's an issue of leadership.' He said he wanted citizens and city staff alike to be more involved in advising and operating the government.

It was as if our editorial board had written his platform. But more than that, he spoke intelligently and easily on whatever we brought up for over an hour without steering the conversation to his stump speech – he was thinking as we were talking, and giving thoughtful answers. We put him on the cover drawn to look like a superhero – the first time in its history *Eye Weekly* had ever endorsed a political candidate.

And when he took the stage at the Bamboo nightclub on the waterfront and hoisted a broom over his head in victory, there were thousands of rapturous, chanting and (frankly) shocked supporters there. In the balcony, a friend looked at me and said, 'This is probably the closest thing I'll ever experience to Trudeaumania.'

Three years later, the transformation that Miller heralded was less than evident to a lot of people. In 2006, he stood in the sunlight outside Downsview subway station next to a map. He was running for re-election, and cruising to victory over uninspiring challengers, but his campaign lacked the thrill and optimism that had carried him to victory in 2003. Miller was still popular – his approval ratings measured as high as 80 per cent – and he would go on to win a majority of the vote in almost every city ward, as strong a mandate as one might ever expect to see in Toronto. Yet the boundless hope that had propelled his long-shot 2003 campaign had given way to a sense of satisfactory inevitability.

If those who had voted against him fearing an extreme NDP-led socialist agenda had grown comfortable with his leadership, then among his strongest supporters there was a mild feeling of disappointment. During an onstage debate sponsored by *Spacing*, for example, I asked him why it was that Lastman had been able to build more kilometres of bike lanes than he had, and the crowd whooped and roared. Anti-poverty activists accused him of neo-liberalism. At one point, Jonathan Goldsbie of the Toronto Public Space Committee told the press Miller was a 'pimp,' because he'd signed an outdoor advertising contract for bus shelters and garbage cans with Astral Media. An article in *Toronto Life* wondered if he was merely a 'visionary plumber.'

At this campaign event, in a bid to create excitement, Miller unveiled 'Transit City,' a map that outlined planned TTC expansion in the coming years. The map was heavy on surface transit – although an expansion of the Sheppard subway east into Scarborough and an already-planned extension of the Spadina subway to York University were there, a new network of rapid 'Busways' and light rail transit lines carried the bulk of the expansionary load. There was no specific funding attached to the plan as a whole – Miller would be asking the province to fund some of the lines, and the TTC would invest in others as money became available.

The press that had gathered for the announcement collectively yawned. We'd already seen a lot of this in various plans and documents, and there was no firm timeline attached to funding.

A reporter from the *Globe and Mail* asked if we'd trekked all the way out to the far end of the subway line in North York just to rehash existing unfunded ideas. 'What's new,' Miller said, 'is we're committing to a city-wide, integrated network of transit, of speedy, reliable service.' Putting it all together as a coordinated plan and then committing to find the money needed to build it was the big news here, Miller said.

I rode the subway back down to city hall with Miller. We were joined by former TTC marketing manager Bob Brent – an admirer of Miller's work on the TTC – and a rotating cast of regular citizens startled and happy to see the mayor on the train with them. They approached Miller throughout the trip to shake his hand, to tell him they were voting for him, to let him know they thought he was doing a good job. Despite this glad-handing, I took the opportunity to ask Miller about the disappointment people were feeling. We'd expected transformation. Where was it?

'That's not what people tell me on the street: people tell me all the time that they're happy, keep it up,' he said. 'I've done pretty much what I said I would. I think people put their hopes in me, and I'm very proud of that, but it's not just about me, it's about Toronto. And I think people share my frustration that Toronto can't succeed the way it should until we've dealt with the leftovers from the Harris era, the downloading and the lack of funding.'

People might be disappointed that he had not turned the city into a network of bike lanes overnight, but he had never promised to make any such radical overhauls. In fact, he'd been clear from the beginning that he thought change came at the street level, slowly, organically. As he repeated to me, it isn't about showpiece megaprojects: 'It's not how you build a city, and it wasn't my vision of building a city three years ago. You don't build monuments. You build a city neighbourhood by neighbourhood. It's an incremental thing, and it should be. Cities are organic, and that's why things like the community safety plan work, because it's about neighbourhoods and about investing in young people in neighbourhoods. That's why Clean and Beautiful works: it's about bringing neighbourhoods together –

the businesses, the people, the city – to make the neighbourhood a more livable place, to make the public space more livable. And that's my philosophy on how you build a city.'

Indeed, the symbolic gesture that had fulfilled his big campaign promise – killing the island airport bridge at his first meeting – put the kibosh on the very notion of grand projects. And much of what he could cite as his most important accomplishments, addressing the infrastructure gaps leftover from Lastman, didn't feature prominently in news reports about city hall. It simply wasn't sexy. Miller and his council implemented a plan to update the sewer system and pay for it with a gradual increase in water fees over the course of twenty-five years. They developed a long-term plan to slow the rate of commercial tax increases to bring them gradually into line with the rates of other GTA cities. Miller campaigned hard – to the annoyance of politicians at other levels of government who thought he should tend his own fiscal garden – to get a 'new deal for cities,' and wound up securing a share of the gas tax from both the province and the feds that amounted to roughly $200 million per year in transit funding. He fully implemented the TTC Ridership Growth strategy that included running buses more frequently and better, and, over the course of his term, saw ridership increase to record levels. He installed a lobbyist registry and integrity commissioner to keep the backrooms free of undue influence. And in the lead-up to his re-election bid, he finally put to rest the long-standing debate about what to do with Toronto's garbage – we'd been shipping it to Michigan and lots of right-wing councillors wanted to incinerate it – by buying a landfill near London, Ontario, and recommitting to a strategy to gradually increase the amount of waste we recycle and compost. The official plan was rewritten to guide the evolution of the city, and, late in his second term, a new harmonized zoning bylaw was passed for the first time since amalgamation.

Perhaps most significantly, Miller persuaded the province to introduce the City of Toronto Act, which would be passed at the tail end of his first term. The legislation was akin to a municipal charter for Canada's largest city: it gave the city more authority to act on its own on a host of local matters; gave the city some leeway to introduce taxes beyond property taxes – including road tolls, vehicle registration and land transfer taxes – and it gave more authority to the mayor's office, allowing him to appoint committee heads in consultation with city council, to establish a governing executive committee to control council's agenda, and to act as the CEO of the city. The legislation stopped short of implementing a 'strong mayor' executive system that would have given Miller the presidential-type powers many U.S. mayors enjoy, but he insisted he did not want such a system. The mayor was a leader, he said, but council ruled the city.

Indeed, although I say Miller did these things, perhaps it's more accurate to say that council did them under his leadership. But for all of Miller's time as mayor, the two concepts seemed synonymous. He never lost a single major vote at city council in his entire two terms as mayor, an accomplishment that in retrospect seems like a masterwork of negotiation and persuasion – and a tribute, perhaps, to his incremental approach.

And incremental or not, the city's real estate prices continued to soar, its streetscapes gentrified and a new category of youngish people seemed ascendant: you could say Toronto experienced a rise of the creative class.

Richard Florida relocated to Toronto in 2007, a year into Miller's second term. In his book *The Rise of the Creative Class*, Florida theorized that 'creative workers' – not just artists and poets but digital tech, media, academic, finance, health care and legal professionals – defined economic success for cities in the post-industrial age. Cities that could attract these professionals would thrive, and those that could not would struggle. The headline-grabbing element of his work – including the much-discussed Bohemian Index and Gay Index – was the idea that a city could reverse-engineer this economic success by becoming the kind of place in which those workers wanted to live. Tolerance of ethnic diversity and pansexual freedom. Walkable, livable neighbourhoods filled with bike lanes. Great mass transit and cool coffee shops. A thriving music and arts scene and brick-and-beam converted warehouse office spaces. If you built cool neighbourhoods, you would attract cool workers, and those cool workers would attract cool companies.

Florida's work, and the enthusiasm with which it was received in the mainstream press, provoked vivid debate about cause and effect, and those who thought he was merely describing the process of gentrification at a city-wide scale – and possibly celebrating and encouraging it through his consulting business – made angry accusations of both a neo-liberal agenda and snake-oil salesmanship. Florida strenuously objected to those criticisms, citing his personal philosophical grounding in Marxism, the detailed numbers in his studies and his own advocacy for ensuring the creative city was one where prosperity was both created and shared by an ever-wider spectrum of the population.

Either way, Florida's landing in Toronto was symbolic, because the first decade of the millennium was most noteworthy for the increased dominance of the creative class in the downtown mainstream of Toronto life. The skyline was transformed, and continues to be transformed, by the construction of hundreds of condominium buildings. New office-tower construction in the core broadened the geography occupied by institutional businesses working in finance and telecommunications. When Telus relocated its offices from the Scarborough Town Centre to the new 'SouthCore' extension of the Financial District in 2009 – the beginning of a rush of large employers moving from the suburbs to the city's heart, paying higher rents to attract the condo-dwellers living nearby – it sounded a chord of Floridian resonance.

Downtown was the place to be. There were new boutique luxury hotels and a new boutique luxury airline at the Island Airport, and a new designer park in condoland with sculptures by zeitgeist-surfer Douglas Coupland. Whole swaths of previously gritty Toronto gentrified rapidly; the spread of high-end espresso shops, artisanal restaurants and 'curated' quirk emporia spread like a contagion east and west, lifting the economic prospects, property values and rents ever higher.

All the creative energy that appeared to be bubbling up in the city just before Miller was first elected exploded onto the street – but now with official civic approval and support. Major landmarks and institutions unveiled a series of new architectural showpieces; the Nuit Blanche and Luminato festivals took over the streets in the name of the arts; Pedestrian Sundays in Kensington Market saw face-painted dancers celebrating environmental themes on closed roadways; Drake, Feist, the Weeknd, K'naan and Fucked Up spearheaded a local dominance of the world pop music scene; the Evergreen Brick Works turned an industrial site in the Don Valley into a massive environmental laboratory/think tank/playground; seemingly a million farmers' markets took over parking lots on summer weekends.

The easiest gig I've ever had was as the Innovation and Job News reporter for the online Toronto economy publication *Yonge Street* toward the end of Miller's second term in office. I had to find three to six innovative, creative-class companies who were hiring or expanding each week. I could have found ten times that many to write about in the digital media and app development industries alone, as Toronto emerged as a global start-up powerhouse behind only New York, London and Silicon Valley. Indeed, the business sector as a whole in Toronto did well under Miller, as GDP grew by more than 10 per cent over the course of the decade, even as the world outside Canada collapsed into recession. According to various surveys released in 2010 and 2011, Toronto had become the 'lowest risk city in the world for employers' (Aon Consulting); the world's sixth 'most business competitive global city' (KPMG); the most livable city in the world (PricewaterhouseCoopers); one of the world's Top 10 on the Global Financial Centres Index; and twelfth in the world on the Global Economic Power Index.

I visited Florida at his office in 2009, and he told me that, in part, he'd been attracted to Toronto precisely because of David Miller's understanding of urbanism. 'Whether you're a civil engineer or a historian, or even a biologist,' Florida said, 'I've never talked to so many people who care about urban systems and urban ecology from so many walks of life. It's like Austin and Nashville are places that have music, L.A. has film, Toronto has urbanism. It's what everybody cares about. And I think there's a Toronto school of urbanism that has a lot to say.'

And, he told me, sitting on the couch in the lobby of his think tank's offices, Toronto was maybe the best example of successful urbanism in the world: 'Toronto is a very good example of a city that has a balance between young people and families – and not just wealthy families. It has wealthy families and low-income families and immigrant families and gay and lesbian families.' When he wrote about the Creative City, he said, Toronto was close to 'an ideal of what I had in mind.' Although Florida didn't think the great global Alpha Cities such as New York and London would lose their dominance, Toronto had an opportunity to be a world leader in defining what a great city could look like: 'We have a continuous city; we don't have a hole in the doughnut, so to speak. Yes, we have segregation and segmentation, but we have a broad-based diversity that is inclusive across gender, race, gay and lesbian, class lines. Yes, it could be better; yes, it's becoming more segmented; but we have to understand how much of an asset that is. The fact that our major universities are in the core is a big deal. Our ravine system – and I think what the folks at the Brick Works are trying to achieve – is a big, big, big deal.'

His comments dovetailed with a boom that appeared to be transforming downtown into a never-ending street festival for the wealthy and the upwardly mobile. But Florida didn't think Toronto was a city without problems, and he told me the growing segregation between the suburbs and the city core as enclaves of low- and high-income people was the No. 1 problem we faced, and that Hulchanski's *Three Cities* report was 'the single most important document written about Toronto.' Following that, the affordability of housing and expanding transit to deal with the 'nightmarish' traffic were at the top of the agenda.

But he had no solutions to those problems. And didn't think the solutions were for him to come up with. 'I learned that from Jane Jacobs,' he said. 'I asked Jane Jacobs what she would do to help after 9/11 in Manhattan, what would be her plan. And she said, "You're asking the wrong question." And I kept asking her, "Well, what would be your plan? What would you do?" She said,

"I don't know. It's what the people who live in that neighbourhood would do, what the shop owners who have shops in that neighbourhood would do, what the people who work in that neighbourhood would do, and it has to be a more collective, organic response." So that's what I would say, that to solve these problems we have to empower the groups – immigrant groups, worker groups, labour groups, agricultural groups – and we have to bring them together in a framework that enables all of us to use our creativity to solve those problems.'

4

One of the counter-narratives to David Miller's 2003 victory was the story of Karen Stintz, a thirty-something professional civil servant from Yonge and Eglinton who had two master's degrees and no political experience. Long-serving ward incumbent Anne Johnston had angered a local residents' group when she approved a new high-rise tower, and in response the group put a gimmicky 'Councillor Wanted' advertisement in the local paper. Stintz answered the ad and decided to run, though the angry residents turned out to have no money to put behind her candidacy. She recruited her husband to serve as campaign manager, set up shop in her living room and started campaigning.

Stintz lost money on her first fundraiser, and over the course of the campaign managed to raise only $17,000 – roughly 30 per cent of the spending limit. It was enough, though, to fund some flyers bearing her photo and signature, and she told me she took those flyers to every single door in the ward. Even though her story of answering the help-wanted ad generated some publicity in the daily papers – hard to come by for an unknown candidate facing a popular incumbent – Johnston never really took Stintz's campaign seriously.

On election day, Stintz won a surprise victory. That night, in his own victory speech, David Miller lamented the loss from council of his political mentor, Johnston, who had been the first councillor to endorse his candidacy. Stintz, a Progressive Conservative party member who had endorsed John Tory in the mayor's race, gave birth just days after the election, but still gamely showed up for work, bringing her baby in tow. She found her council colleagues supportive of her maternity situation, but got a chilly reception from the new mayor. 'He wouldn't even talk to me,' she said.

While Lastman's agenda was set by lobbyists and he governed through horse-trading and intimidation, he also shrewdly kept his enemies as close as his friends. (Even Miller himself, when a councillor in the Lastman administration, served on the transit commission and chaired the city's working group on immigrant and refugee issues.) Vocal opponents of Miller's got no such quarter in his administration. It wasn't that he wouldn't work with conservatives – he appointed card-carrying Tory David Soknaki as his first-term budget chief, for example – but he assembled a coalition to govern and maintained that coalition rather than seeking support outside of it. In his office, I once asked Miller about this and he saw it a bit differently. Councillors like Denzil Minnan-Wong only wanted to oppose him, he said, and weren't interested in working productively: 'I can propose something Denzil himself proposed last week and suddenly he'll be against it.'

In any event, he didn't need the support of Stintz and the hardcore right-wing. Miller's opponents flailed around ineffectively, unable to even adequately present a competing argument in public against his proposals, never mind defeat them. During Miller's second term, Stintz and Case Ootes tried to bring some coherence to the opposition and formed the Responsible Government Group. That organization was no more effective. And in retrospect, the most interesting fact of the group's existence was the conspicuous absence among its members of city hall's most visible conservative: Rob Ford, city council's angry, blustering loner, out pounding the pavement in the suburbs.

5

When Richard Florida and Rob Ford agree on something, it's wise to pay attention. Both men, in their various ways, were aware that the inner suburbs dramatically upended Toronto's narrative of growth and prosperity. Florida saw them as one of the city's greatest challenges and Ford talked about how the very diverse, mostly low-income neighbourhoods of his ward were crying out for attention, that they were alienated from the downtown chatter about bike lanes and the waterfront. And by the end of Miller's first term, Hulchanski's *Three Cities* report and the United Way's Strong Neighbourhoods Task Force had provided the data to fuel the concerns, both insisting that the city needed to pay attention to its peripheral regions.

I had some sense of the challenge the suburbs presented, because, off and on, I'd lived in the heart of Scarborough for fifteen years. It was the place I became an adult. My parents still live out there, near Markham and Lawrence. Five years ago, I went back, to study exactly what we talk about when we talked about the suburbs as the new inner city. I stood on the sidewalk, watching the blur of twelve lanes of cars and trucks cruising past at eighty kilometres an hour. I noted the vast parking lots that dominated three of the corners (the fourth was home to a gas station and a drive-through Tim Horton's), expanses of asphalt larger than most downtown city blocks. There were almost no other pedestrians in sight. The scale of the neighbourhood, as I knew well from my youth, was alienating.

I reminded myself that 73 per cent of people in Toronto live in the inner suburbs, very many of them at places like Markham and Lawrence. At David Miller's city hall, people spoke often – at practically every press conference – of Toronto as a 'city of neighbourhoods.' But for a majority of Torontonians, this is what their neighbourhood looked like. And according to the 2006 census, about 30 per cent of households in the neighbourhood were classified as low-income (15 per cent were high-income). Slightly less than 60 per cent of residents were immigrants, and more than half of those had arrived in Canada after 1980; 68.5 per cent were visible minorities (with substantial Indian, Sri Lankan, Chinese, Filipino, Jamaican and African populations); more than a fifth of the population was under age fifteen. Just by way of comparison, the Annex, Jane Jacobs' former neighbourhood and one of the celebrated examples of Toronto's village-within-a-city utopianism, had about 30 per cent fewer low-income residents, was 70 per cent Canadian-born and 80 per cent white, and only 7.6 per cent of its residents were children under fifteen.

This contrast was increasingly evident in the reports comparing Toronto's central area to its inner suburbs. According to the United Way's *Poverty by Postal Code*, based on the 2001 census, the former municipality of Toronto – what we now call downtown – had gotten richer in the decade between 1991 and 2001, while every one of the other former municipalities had grown poorer: 'By 2001, the former cities of York, North York and Scarborough all had poverty levels where more than one in every five of their families were living in poverty.' Using 2006 census data, David Hulchanski made the same point all the more vivid in an update of *Three Cities Within Toronto*. From 1970 to 2006, the number of areas considered 'middle-income' – which we might think of as mixed-income neighbourhoods – had shrunk dramatically, from 66 per cent to only 29 per cent. Hulchanski put his finger on why this posed a problem for the city's vulnerable residents: 'In the 1970s, most of the city's low-income neighbourhoods were in the inner city. This meant that low-income households had good access to transit and services. Some of these neighbourhoods have gentrified and are now home to affluent households, while low-income households are concentrated in the northeastern and northwestern parts of the city (the inner suburbs), with relatively poor access to transit and services.' I got to see first-hand, in my own life, what that difference in access looked like.

I always say my parents live at Markham and Lawrence. But, really, I mean near Markham and Lawrence – near in the sense that people in Scarborough mean it. Markham and Lawrence is the closest major intersection to where my folks live – though it's roughly a two-kilometre trip from their house to that corner. (For downtown-dwellers, approximately the distance from the ferry docks to Ryerson University.) In Scarborough, that distance is considered very close. It's a place where you're tempted to – and often do – take a bus to the nearest major intersection (and even at that, the walk from my parents' house to the bus stop is greater than the distance between King and Queen subway stations). The sprawling scale of the neighbourhood is hard to overstate, and the question of distance is not insignificant to the discussion of Markham and Lawrence or of Scarborough or the inner suburbs more generally. When you're discussing proximity in Scarborough, you can take one measuring stick of neighbourhood livability – how much is within a ten-minute walk of one's home? – and replace the word *walk* with *drive*.

We moved to Markham and Lawrence from the not-yet-gentrifying neighbourhood of South Riverdale – now known as Riverside – in 1986, when I was fourteen. At the time, our three-bedroom, two-storey Victorian row house at Broadview and Gerrard was pretty much a straight-up swap, price-wise, for our four-bedroom Scarborough bungalow. (We moved from the neighbourhood my father and I spent our entire lives in mostly because we couldn't afford a bigger house in Riverdale.) Since Scarborough has been virtually left out of the real estate booms of the past two decades, an offer to trade back would not be accepted today.

In South Riverdale, my parents had been active members of the community at St. Ann's Catholic Church, the doors of which were exactly 176 twelve-year-old paces from our front porch. I walked with my siblings to school about five minutes south on Boulton Avenue. My dad worked, for a long while, as a department store manager a ten-minute walk east at Carlaw. My paternal grandfather and three of his siblings (and therefore many of my cousins) lived in various houses within a few blocks of our place, and we'd often wander around visiting. In the winter, we'd go tobogganing at Riverdale Park at the end of the block. On the way home from school, we'd ride the swings at a tiny parkette in the middle of Boulton Avenue, and later in the evening my brother and I would walk to Pape Recreation Centre for swimming lessons. For a long time my parents didn't own a car, so we'd take the streetcar for fifteen minutes to get to hockey games or to go to the movies at Yonge and Dundas. We knew many, many people within a five- or ten-minute walk of our house, and our social life existed almost entirely in the neighbourhood.

Things were not unpleasant when we moved to Markham and Lawrence, but they were different. We had a backyard almost the size of that Boulton Avenue parkette that was good for kicking a ball around in, as well as a front yard and a grassy boulevard, too. There was a hundred-foot-long driveway that my brother and I played basketball and road hockey in, but we never made any friends who lived within pickup-game walking distance of our house. We had a big garage with a loft above it, and we had two bathrooms. The neighbours a few doors down had kids the same age as my two youngest siblings, and they'd all run around on the sidewalks playing together. The new subdivision of quiet, winding cul-de-sacs and crescents was a far superior bicycle joyriding course to the congested streets in the city. Most notably, I did not have to share a bedroom with my two brothers.

But there were downsides. The trip to my Catholic high school on the Scarborough Bluffs involved twenty minutes of walking and a fifteen-minute bus ride. A trip to the variety store was best made in a car. We were on smiling terms with our immediate neighbours (and one of them was on lecturing-about-our-leaves-blowing-into-his-backyard terms with us), but the relationships were more civil than social. When, as a teenager, I got involved with a girl who also lived 'at' Markham and Lawrence, the walk to her house (which I made three or four times a week until she got a car) took about forty-five minutes. I have a lot of very happy memories from the time I lived at Markham and Lawrence, but unlike my memories of earlier childhood, very few of them are tied to anything about the neighbourhood we lived in outside the walls of my parents' house. (Exceptions: the ravine nearby was an excellent spot for underage drinking and budding romance, and I had fun at one of my first jobs at National Sports Centre in the Cedarbrae Mall.) And a huge number of my memories of that time, good and bad, involve long, lonely walks into the wind, impatient waits for buses and extended interior monologues about the monotony of the suburbs.

According to the City of Toronto, Markham and Lawrence is part of a neighbourhood called Woburn. The name was taken from the Woburn Inn, which stood at what is today Markham Road and Painted Post, just a little north of Lawrence. The Woburn Inn was the original site of Scarborough's municipal government, chosen for its geographic centrality, though the area around it was almost completely undeveloped. It remained the town hall for seventy-one years, until 1921. That's a neat tidbit of local history in a place that has little remarkable history at all, and no doubt worthy of commemoration. But the very idea of the neighbourhood of Woburn is fiction.

For one thing, the city draws Woburn's jagged neighbourhood boundaries at approximately Ellesmere in the north and the CNR tracks north of Eglinton in the south, at McCowan Road in the west and Orton Park Road in the east. That's an area roughly fourteen kilometres square, or two-thirds the size of the former municipality of East York. It has a population just over 53,000, making it as populous as Fredericton, New Brunswick. To call an area that large a neighbourhood is simply absurd.

Furthermore, if you ask people who live near Markham and Lawrence what life in Woburn is like, they will not recognize that you are talking about their home. Most would recognize the name as belonging to a high school a fifteen-minute drive north, but even there the name's not commonly applied to the surrounding area. They just don't call it that. In fact, they don't call it anything, really, except Markham and Lawrence. The city's Strong Neighbourhoods Task Force outlined this problem as part of their study of Woburn: 'One resident noted that he did not value anything in the neighbourhood "because it wasn't a neighbourhood."' He represented 25 per cent of the total resident respondents to their survey.

The real neighbourhood around Markham and Lawrence – still large in downtown terms, but maybe a quarter the size of the city's official demarcations – might be called Cedarbrae. The local commercial centre, to the extent that there is one, is Cedarbrae Mall. The local high school next door is Cedarbrae Collegiate. The busy library across the street is Cedarbrae Library. Still, no one I met while I lived there or afterwards ever called the neighbourhood that. Save for its street names, Markham and Lawrence remains, in effect, nameless.

To fill in some details about what it's like, though: outside of Cedarbrae, almost all of the commercial development is in strip malls with parking lots in front of them. There are several dozen of these. The significant geographic landmark is a sprawling forest and ravine – the Highland Creek – running alongside and across Markham Road south of Lawrence.

The residential development is split almost evenly between detached bungalows and high-rise apartment towers. The blocks immediately north and southwest of Markham and Lawrence are made up of winding roads lined with modest, fully detached bungalows and the odd split-level home. These homes are on uniformly large lots with yards both in back and front. The uniformity extends to the architecture of the houses, which varies imperceptibly, if at all, from house to house.

To the west, along Lawrence, and to the southeast, the blocks are made up of clusters of concrete apartment towers built in the unremarkable late-fifties brown-box-with-balconies style. These are also situated on winding streets and most are surrounded by lakes of green grass stretching out to chain-link fences that meet the sidewalk, giving the drab towers an isolated feel even in a densely populated block. These towers are home to the most impoverished and low-income residents, those most drastically affected by the neighbourhood's increasingly evident drawbacks. Many have rents that are government-subsidized. This is true especially of the southeast block, which was among the census tracts identified as being 'at risk' in the 2004 *Poverty by Postal Code* report.

Glenn De Baeremaeker, the city councillor for the part of the area west of Markham Road, acknowledged to me in 2007 that the neighbourhood is a planning 'disaster.' De Baeremaeker is a man who rides his bicycle for an hour and a bit to city hall every day (he may be the only such man in Scarborough). 'Urban and intense and beautiful and charming,' he said, 'all the things that we would want today in a neighbourhood, it is not.' And yet, in the next breath, De Baeremaeker went out of his way to point out that it is not a neighbourhood of automatons: 'In a lot of ways, it is a strong neighbourhood. The vibrancy that's here is amazing.'

To see that vibrancy, you need to get away from the broad roads and parking lots. You need to get inside. Five years ago, the available retail options were dazzlingly eclectic and multi-cultural. At the Soon Lee Supermarket in the super-strip mall on the northeast corner, for example, there was a bustling Chinese grocery, stocked with all manner of exotica: bitter melons, which look like cucumbers cross-bred with porcupines; malanga lila, like turnips with hair; dried seaweed; exotic dried mushrooms; and pickled bamboo shoots. The aisles were constantly full of people, and at the checkout local newspapers were available in five non-English languages. The shops neighbouring Soon Lee included Spice It Up Caribbean Cuisine, the Bollywood 4 U video shop and East End Beauty Supplies, which specialized in straightening products for black women's hair. In the Danforth Food Market, an outlet for South Asian and East and West Indian food, aisle three was designated 'Yam/Cane Food/Oil/Sugar/Hot Sauce/Soap.'

Down south of Lawrence, in another strip mall, there was an Islamic store-of-all-trades advertising Afghani bread for seventy-five cents. Inside there was a halal takeout counter, a butcher, a film processing window, a grocery store, as well as china, rugs and non-representational art. A block east, in another strip mall, there was a large sari boutique, its windows filled with bright, shiny orange, green and pink fabrics.

To be sure, there were plenty of corporate chains – three Tim Horton's franchises and two Dollaramas within a block of the intersection, for example, and two Telus mobility shops inside the mall alone. Cedarbrae Mall, to be honest, was fairly pathetic by mall standards, especially in its four-shop food court. It had evolved from a long narrow strip plaza, and it remained little more than a long, narrow hall of stores, with none of the faux landscaping or constructed commercial squares and fountains of places like the Eaton Centre. But the Loblaws, for all that it was just a Loblaws, dwarfed the locations downtown and offered organics, health foods and a truly impressive fresh fish counter.

In the foyer of Cedarbrae Collegiate just south of the mall, you could see and hear students from more than sixty countries, wearing not just the baggy-jeans uniform of teenagers across the continent but also turbans and, in a few cases, a full niqab. The school had a football team like most, but it also had a translation club, made up of students who translate school documents into more than twenty-five languages.

You could, and can, as De Baeremaeker says, find a thriving culture. And the people inside the shops and schools and restaurants seem to be parts of thriving ethnic subcultures, everyone a short drive from a community they feel a part of. Yet the scale and layout of the neighbourhood means you don't find what you don't know you're looking for. To get to the Chinese supermarket, say, you need to get in your car, parked in your driveway, and drive to a parking spot directly in front of the store. There is very little of what Jacobs called the 'random interaction' of the urban environment. Everyone is separated by lanes of cars and acres of barren space. It's segregation by suburban design.

The joint United Way–City of Toronto Strong Neighbourhoods Task Force report that studied Woburn at the end of Lastman's term reads like a catalogue of desolation: 'As part of their explanation of why they did not feel Woburn was a neighbourhood, participants described some general characteristics of a neighbourhood. They described neighbourhood as a place of belonging, an area where people knew one another (or knew of one another). Neighbourhoods implied familiarity and relationships. Neighbourhoods were seen as areas where people walked and where local services, like schools, neighbourhood parks, banks and local food stores, were available.' Markham and Lawrence failed on almost all counts.

There's more. The report describes it as a neighbourhood with few, if any, focal points or public spaces. Despite statistics that say otherwise, many residents feel as if they live in a crime-ridden, unsafe ghetto. The neighbourhood's two parks – one of which sprawls thirty-one acres along the ravine and features picnic grounds, toboggan runs and volleyball courts – are assets. But they're hidden, accessible only by pathways through residential subdivisions, and function primarily as yards for those whose houses back onto them. Similarly, outside of a city-run crafts workshop on Confederation Drive, culture has little presence here. The lone movie theatre closed down in the great multiplex purge of the 1990s; there are no galleries, theatres, music halls or even dance clubs. The nearest athletic recreational facility, containing an ice rink and a rec pool, is a fifteen-minute drive away. There's nowhere remotely close, even by Scarborough's elastic definition of that word, where a gymnasium is available for public use. When I investigated in 2007, the nearest public health office was twenty minutes away by car (double that by public transit). The nearest Canada Employment office was at the Scarborough Town Centre, a half-hour trip by transit (if you're lucky and the bus connections work). Worse, for an unemployed single mother (just under a third of Woburn's families have only one parent) with no car, the closest Ontario Works (that is, welfare) office was at Finch and Neilson, a trip that can take more than half an hour by transit. Community service organizations intended to serve the neighbourhood's population were only located in other regions of Scarborough, thirty to forty minutes away by public transit.

'The sad part of this is that this wasn't created this way by mistake or by neglect,' De Baeremaeker told me. 'These were purposeful decisions by the smartest, brightest urban planners of the 1960s. We purposely did this, and now we're saying, "My God, what a disaster."' At the Cedarbrae Library, when I visited in 2007, they sold several volumes of local history. (If you asked to buy one, the librarian looked at you as though you'd asked for an order of fish and chips, and joked about the dust as she finally handed you your selections.) One of these, *A History of Scarborough*, published originally in 1965, contained side-by-side aerial photos of Markham and Lawrence from 1954 and 1962. In the 1954 photo, there are thirteen houses and what appears to be a church within a block of the intersection. These scattered residences are surrounded entirely by farmland. In the photo taken eight years later, the area looks very much like it does today. There's Cedarbrae Mall, and the school and library; there's the semicircular strip plaza on the northeast corner and there's the gas station. The winding subdivisions of housing are complete to the north and southwest. Six of the eventual dozen apartment towers are already up. While there are still patches of green in the photo that have been paved or built on (or both) in the decades since, to an astonishing degree, the neighbourhood in 1962 was as it is today. The photo evidence shows that, eight years before the Beatles' first single, a rural farming community was entirely erased and replaced with a fully formed suburb.

The book's prose is breathless about the transformation: 'With the close of the War in 1945, the return from overseas and marriage of men of the Armed Forces, and the influx into Canada of hosts of immigrants from Europe, Scarborough opened a new and amazing chapter in her history. During the next twenty years farm after farm was quickly devoured by the bulldozers and subdividers; row upon row of closely packed houses and towering apartment buildings took possession of the former wide fields; great factories sprang up in green pastures.' Scarborough, a sleepy township of 25,000, became 'Ontario's fifth largest municipality and one of the great industrial and commercial centers of Canada, enriched by the skills of men of many nations ... Where the white frame house of Scarborough's first Reeve, Peter Secor, stood amid open fields as late as 1959 at the junction of the Markham Road and Lawrence, today great plazas, lit with brilliant neon lights, are thronged with thousands of shoppers every Thursday and Friday night.'

There are pages devoted to the structural, administrative and financial resources that went into meeting the challenges of the exponentially multiplying population: the infrastructure building, the reformation of the tax code and structure of municipal government, the massive investment in schools. ('No effort or expense was being spared in the attempt to provide [youth] with the best modern educational opportunities possible.')

It was built as a suburban paradise, according to the planning orthodoxy of the time (clear separation between commercial and residential areas; wide major roads to allow for high-speed travel; winding subdivisions with limited access to major streets to prevent through traffic on residential roads). The result, as De Baeremaeker said: 'I think if you were able to go back in time to 1964 and talk to the local city councillors and city planners and local merchants, they'd all talk about how magnificent it was.

The people who built that were proud of what they did. There was a suburban dream where the car was a saviour. It's almost a monument to the automobile. A very ugly monument, but a monument nonetheless.'

Such planning has, of course, been discredited for its environmental crimes and isolating effects, and the market's demonstrated a preference for a downtown model. Today, a three-bedroom house in High Park costs far more than a mansion on the Scarborough Bluffs. When I spoke to the mayors of the GTA suburbs of Markham and Ajax in 2011, they told me they were moving to pedestrianize their cities. Mississauga mayor Hazel McCallion has called the car-centric planning of the city she's ruled for decades a mistake, and the mayor of Vaughan, Maurizio Bevilacqua, loudly trumpets the parking-free development springing up around the planned subway stop in his suburban municipality's new downtown core. A 2012 study by the Royal Bank and the Pembina Institute showed that 80 per cent of GTA residents would prefer to live in a modest dwelling in a walkable area than in a large house on a large lot in a car-dependent area. (Why, then, does suburban sprawl continue? Simple: '79 per cent choose to live where they do based on the cost of the home.')

But the original population moving into Scarborough in droves bought into that 1960s dream, and for a time it served its suburban purpose. But the problem is, it's not a suburb anymore.

'[These neighbourhoods] have a weakness,' De Baeremaeker said, 'and that weakness has become overtly glaring in the last twenty years ... If you're renting in a high-rise building and you don't have a car and you don't own a cottage for your kids to go to in the summer, then what's here? We are becoming a more urban place and it's not working. And we need to change it.'

But it's easier to build a community in eight years than it is to unbuild it in twenty. The commercial developments are owned by landlords who have invested millions and are making millions more. The apartment towers are by now mortgage-free and generating huge profits. Those inconvenient, winding subdivisions are, as always, filled with people who are happy to have been able to afford a patch of green where they can barbecue on the weekends. Turning this suburban community into what De Baeremaeker envisions as an 'urban village' will take significantly longer – twenty-five to thirty years in his estimation. And that's if the residents there ever agree that such a transformation is possible – or worth it.

6

Even if it would take a generation or two, bringing vitality and prosperity to the inner suburbs was much on David Miller's mind while he was mayor. In fact, he considered the inner suburbs the forefront of his agenda. Miller's critics always accused him of harbouring a secret plan to implement road tolls (and his loudest supporters often hoped he did), but he said that it would be unfair to implement road pricing. Many of the city's most vulnerable people lived in the suburbs, he said, and they depended on cars because public transit did not serve them well. To ask those people to start paying a premium to drive without first giving them the viable option of using the TTC would be an injustice.

Bringing the TTC to those far corners of the city was behind the Transit City plan Miller introduced at Downsview Station that afternoon on the campaign trail in 2006. Though the plan changed by the time it was given funding by the province in 2007 and became more of a building plan than a campaign platform, the emphasis behind the LRT plan remained bringing rapid transit to the northeastern and northwestern corners of the city. LRT was affordable enough that we could build a lot of it relatively quickly, and a lot of fast transit, as soon as possible, was what the suburbs desperately needed.

Miller also introduced a strategy that focused on putting both community and specialized police resources into thirteen so-called priority neighbourhoods located in the inner suburbs. Grants for youth programs and anti-poverty programs flowed into these areas. Parks and public facilities were built. Miller always called the program one of his 'core values.' The East Scarborough Storefront in the Kingston-Galloway neighbourhood of

Scarborough is one example of the policy in action. Housed in a former police station, the space acts as a social-service hub for the area, providing job-search help, immigrant landing services, a boys and girls club, and food programs. It coordinates the services of more than thirty-five non-profit and government agencies, and administers the local Tower Renewal project. That initiative harnesses over four hundred local volunteers in an effort to rebuild the community in a tower block along Lawrence, making tenants partners with their landlords and converting local stretches of asphalt into green space, and challenging local youth to work with professional architects to create 'spectacular architecture' to develop the neighbourhood. 'The idea is that if residents have ideas to improve their neighbourhood,' Storefront director Anne Gloger told the *Toronto Observer* in 2012, 'we work with them. We work with anyone and everyone who wants to improve the economic well-being of the neighbourhood. Our vision is to create a thriving community economically, socially and environmentally.'

Anyone who spoke regularly to Miller at any point in his term would have heard of his Tower Renewal program. Toronto's immense building boom in the 1960s generated more than a thousand concrete-slab apartment towers, more than any other city except New York. St. Jamestown, on the edge of Cabbagetown, might be the most visible and prominent, but the majority of these towers were built in the inner suburbs. By the mid-2000s, they were in dire straits: crumbling, energy-inefficient, the alienation of their isolated 'tower-in-a-park' construction evident, and increasingly home to concentrations of the city's poorest citizens. For Miller, the revitalization project tied together several of the core values he was always talking about. Tower Renewal proposed green-energy retrofits of the aging buildings that would both improve their structural soundness and aesthetics and that would finance themselves with conservation savings. The program also included the construction of new infill housing and commercial development in the tower neighbourhoods, alongside redevelopment of local parks and community service amenities, and the introduction of local urban agriculture and improved transportation infrastructure. It was, as Miller said again and again, about making both the towers themselves and the communities they served stronger, about creating both economic and environmental sustainability, and giving the residents the infrastructure they needed to increase the vibrancy of their own neighbourhoods.

'It's a way that we can make Toronto more livable and prosperous, with opportunity for every single Torontonian,' Miller said when he launched the program in 2008. The program kicked off with four pilot projects, including St. Jamestown and sites in North York, Scarborough and Etobicoke, with a plan to extend it, over time, to every tower neighbourhood in the city.

Transit City, Tower Renewal and priority neighbourhood investment – if you asked Miller, these things would stand as his legacy, projects that bound together community strength and economic and environmental sustainability, and sought to spread the prosperity and community vitality so evident downtown to every corner of the city. Fixing the post-amalgamation disarray of the city's governance defined his first term. Addressing the physical and community infrastructure deficit felt most keenly in the inner suburbs was the overriding project of his second term. He repeatedly said as much to me and to other reporters. But that is not the story now told most frequently about David Miller's time in office. Instead, we hear about strikes, customer service problems, new taxes and the 'War on the Car,' right?

The TTC experienced steady ridership growth but often seemed, at the front-line level, to forget that the system existed to serve riders. Stories abounded about fare collectors and drivers being rude or dismissive to customers (which was frequently my own experience). The system itself underscored this impression by failing to meet schedules – you'd wait for twenty minutes in the cold and then four buses piggybacking each other would arrive all at once. If one passenger failed to show his student fare card, the entire vehicle, sometimes full of hundreds of people, would be forced to wait at a standstill until police arrived to mediate the dispute. Mounting public outrage coalesced around a few symbolic lapses in customer service, most notably when a rider photographed a subway fare collector asleep on the job.

Similar frustrations surrounded a protracted garbage strike in 2009, during which the city's parks were clogged with waste for weeks. Miller, who had long drawn major support from organized labour, ended a sick-day system that allowed workers to save up unused sick leave and take it in the form of cash when they retired. The city's two largest unions, representing both inside and outside workers, fought bitterly. The result was a public relations disaster for both the unions and for Miller, especially when the resolution, a phasing-out of the system rather than a cancellation of it, appeared to the public like a capitulation on the part of the mayor. Miller saw his astronomical approval numbers fall to 29 per cent, and the public turned even further on unions they already regarded as out of touch and entitled.

Other moments of bureaucratic bungling and apparent entitlement piled up as quickly as the garbage. A simple pilot project that allowed vendors to serve street food other than hot dogs was fouled up largely because of the micromanagement of Miller's health commissioner. A major donor to his council speaker Sandra Bussin's campaign had a contract with the city renewed against the advice of staff, and Miller stood steadfastly beside her as she shrugged off accusations over the affair. Meanwhile, tiny but symbolic spending of tax money on penny-ante expenses – always highlighted by a red-faced rant from Rob Ford – created an impression of entitlement: Bussin charged a bunny costume for an Easter Parade to her office budget, Adam Vaughan bought a $200 espresso maker for his office and, most famously, Kyle Rae used a government-subsidized campaign surplus to throw himself a $12,000 retirement party.

A more sobering note was struck when the G20 meetings, foisted by the feds on the city in the summer of 2010, turned into a fiasco. First, violent, vandalizing protesters were permitted to run wild across the downtown core, and then hundreds of peaceful protesters were subsequently rounded up and held in small pens for days, some of them needlessly beaten on camera. It was, institutionally, another no-win situation, as some felt the police should be blamed for not preventing the vandalism and others felt the police should be blamed for the brutality and human-rights violations. From any angle, though, it seemed like a deeply troubling mismanagement of a major event. Commenters called it an enduring black mark on the city's permanent record, but Police Chief Bill Blair defended his officers and admitted no wrongdoing. Miller stood by him, leading council to vote to congratulate the police service on a job well done.

A final example: the St. Clair streetcar right-of-way had been, inadvisably, pitched by Miller as an example of how LRT could transform the city. Again and again, he talked about how we were getting something that would act like a half-capacity subway bought for a tenth the price. But the streetcar was never planned in a way that would allow it to operate as a subway-like LRT; the stops were spaced close together and the vehicles stopped at red lights every half-block. In retrospect, the ROW brought reliability to the streetcar service and helped revitalize street life in many parts of the strip, but selling it as a new-age LRT and vigorously trying to drown out vocal opposition clouded any good impressions of the high-capacity, high-speed LRT lines in Miller's Transit City. It also didn't help that, because of both lawsuits filed by local business owners opposed to the ROW and tragically bad planning by various overlapping government departments, construction took two years longer than expected (snarling traffic in midtown for years) and cost almost twice as much as budgeted.

Which leads us to the War on the Car. This phrase, much bandied about by Miller's opponents and finally embraced on the campaign trail by both Rocco Rossi and Rob Ford, initially used the example of the St. Clair ROW as evidence that a preference for surface transit punished car and truck drivers, and then applied the same logic to Miller's much rumoured, never evident fondness for road tolls.

And then, most dramatically, it was applied to bike lanes. Many cyclists in the city – not to mention many environmentalists, urbanists and transit activists – would have been very happy if Miller had engaged in a War on the Car, but they never saw any evidence of one. When I asked Miller during the 2006 election campaign, why, given all of his rhetoric about the importance of bikes, he had managed to install fewer bike lanes in Toronto during his first term than Mel Lastman had, he explained that the lanes installed under the previous administration, largely at the behest of councillors such as Jack Layton, were the 'easy wins.' In areas of the city where there was broad community support for bike lanes and where the roads were wide enough to easily accommodate them without major changes to traffic flow, the lanes were installed because there was virtually no opposition to them. But to build further, to complete a cycling network across the city, both connecting the downtown patchwork of routes to each other and building out into more traditionally car-dependent areas of the city, was hard work. He claimed to be doing that work, carefully and consistently, to build institutional and political support.

It became clear just how hard that political battle was in 2009, when city council voted to add bike lanes to the downtown route of Jarvis Street. Jarvis was a five-lane road, with an oddball lane in the centre used for southbound traffic in the morning and northbound in the evening. It had long been a major car-traffic artery into the downtown core for the largely affluent residents of midtown and north Toronto. The city and residents groups were concerned that the highway-like design and use of the street had kept it from realizing its potential as a grand avenue – Jarvis was lined by old mansions and surrounded by high residential and commercial density, but the high-speed street traffic was a community killer. (The resulting lack of street life had long made it home to Toronto's most prominent prostitutes' stroll.)

In consultation with local residents and business owners over a period of years, the city came up with a strategy to remove the centre, reversible car lane and broaden the sidewalks to make the area more vibrant for pedestrians, with trees and planter boxes on the newly widened road. Models showed that car trips down the street might lengthen from eight minutes to ten, a small inconvenience for spurring commercial and community vitality on the strip. Then, on its way to council, the plan was tweaked slightly, and some of the space devoted to wider sidewalks was given to cyclists. The move had broad support among local residents, many of whom were cyclists, was made at the request of the local councillor and got the full-throated endorsement of the mayor.

With the initiative before council, seven and a half hours of debate ensued, during which councillors Karen Stintz, Denzil Minnan-Wong and Mike Del Grande decried the move as a 'War on the Car.' And Councillor Ford, on the record as having the opinion that bikes did not belong on the street and that cyclists were responsible for their own deaths because they got in the way, said that bike lanes were a 'pain in the ass.' About a hundred helmet-wearing cyclists in the council chamber applauded as the initiative passed by a vote of twenty-eight to sixteen.

For these activists, heretofore disappointed by Miller's failure to live up to his promises, it was an important symbolic victory. But the headlines the next day focused only on the War on the Car rhetoric, obscuring the fact that the fifth lane on Jarvis had been slated for removal anyway, and giving prominent voice to the critics' complaints that suburban drivers would be inconvenienced at the expense of bike-riding downtowners.

The final front in the imagined War on the Car narrative emerged out of one of Miller's greatest victories. Ever since amalgamation, the city's budget had been a mess, plagued by a 'structural deficit' that left the city with a massive shortfall in revenue every year compared to its expenses. During Lastman's term, the technique for balancing the budget and closing that deficit – as the city needed to do each year since it could not by law borrow to fund operating expenses – had been to beg for a bailout from the provincial government and defer infrastructure maintenance.

Thus began a culture of complaint by voices from all the parties in Ottawa and at Queen's Park that Toronto needed to grow up and handle its own affairs, or 'get its fiscal house in order,' as John Tory put it in his 2003 campaign. As mentioned, Miller did this in various, relentless ways, going so far as to demand that a portion of the GST be given to cities. But he did not simply wait around for the upper levels of government to rain money on the city. He tightened the city's belt – even as new spending was introduced to increase TTC ridership and build social infrastructure across the city, programs were cut, departments shrunk and a never-ending quest for more efficient ways to run the administration was pursued.

And then, most dramatically and controversially, Miller and his second-term budget chief, Shelley Carroll, proposed using two of the tools permitted in the new City of Toronto Act to stabilize the city's finances. A graduated land transfer tax of up to 2 per cent – equivalent to the existing provincial land transfer tax – would draw revenue from the city's booming real estate market. There was an exemption for first-time homebuyers, and while the tax could be steep in dollar terms, it was mild compared to the total purchase price of a home and should have been theoretically absorbed into the price structure of the continually escalating market. And there was always the consolation that the annual property taxes on a $500,000 house in Toronto were about $3,000 cheaper than those in nearby Ajax, and $1,000 less than in Vaughan, Mississauga, Oakville or Markham. And unlike a property tax increase, it would not force working-class people and senior citizens living in houses they purchased before their neighbourhoods gentrified and property values went up to move because of new tax bills.

The other new revenue tool Miller proposed, returning to the War on the Car, was a $60 Vehicle Registration Tax. Through the fare box, transit users in Toronto already pay about 80 per cent of that infrastructure's operating costs. A year's worth of Metropasses costs more than $1,200. By contrast, an average car driver pays about $600 per year in gas taxes, the vast majority of which goes to the provincial and federal governments. A $60-per-car-per-year fee, it was argued, was a small but significant contribution to funding the city's infrastructure that, at $5 per month, would not even cripple low-income drivers. It also had a progressive element: those with no car would pay nothing. As war measures go, it was a mild one.

Together, the new taxes were estimated to generate more than $300 million per year in new revenue – and they wound up generating far more than that. Their implementation, however, raised hell among the council opposition led by Stintz et al. The mayor's opponents managed to win a vote delaying the approval of the new taxes for several months – time, they hoped, to galvanize public opinion. Alongside right-wing tax-cutting organizations and realtors worried the land transfer tax would slow the market, they launched a summer-long public relation campaign. They ramped up the War on the Car rhetoric and characterized the move as an attempt to pick the pockets of car-bound suburban seniors for the benefit of rich downtown cyclists. In fact, the summer of 2007, when the VRT vote was looming, was the first time I saw the headline 'Toronto's war on the car,' in a report by the *National Post*'s Kelly Patrick, who claimed the Miller administration was 'looking to essentially punish motorists out of their automobiles.'

Miller responded angrily, with a scaremongering, cost-cutting proposal that would save $100 million but would require shutting down the entire Sheppard subway line and several suburban bus routes, and the closure of libraries, community centres and recreation facilities. He had the city manager, Shirley Hoy, begin implementing $34 million of these cuts in August without authorization from council. When councillors balked, Miller threatened a massive property tax increase. His obvious gambit: dramatize the budget shortfall by threatening services and gain public support for the new revenue tools. He was confident that, faced with a stark realization of what was at stake, Torontonians would choose to pay more to preserve services rather than allow the proposed cuts to be implemented.

It paid off. At a meeting in September 2007, after eight hours of acrimonious shouting before a full public gallery in the council chamber, council voted to approve both taxes. But before patting Miller on the back too hard for his political savvy, we should note that the move backfired in some respects, too: it divided council, began ramping up the suburban-car-driver versus downtown-elitist rhetoric and, ironically, underscored the public impression that Toronto was teetering on the edge of bankruptcy. To engage the willingness to save transit and libraries, the impression that those things were one council vote away from being shuttered was hammered home.

That's ironic because, alongside the other measures Miller had worked so strenuously on over the years, the new revenue tools lifted the city to within sight of long-term fiscal stability. When the city closed the books on its 2008 spending, it showed a small surplus. When 2009's spending was complete, the surplus was up to $181 million. Miller's final budget, tallied after he'd been out of office for several months, showed a surplus of more than $350 million. Although the projected budgets each year still started with a structural shortfall that sometimes looked staggering, the actual spending – and in particular the revenue generated by the land transfer tax – had pretty much closed the gap. The city's capital debt was orders of magnitude lower, on a per-capita basis, than that of other major cities in the world, and lower than that of Montreal or Vancouver. Our property taxes remained the lowest in the region and lower than in cities like New York, Chicago and Montreal. And the operating budget was now showing healthy surpluses even as services were expanded, year after year.

From the any rational viewpoint, the city's fiscal house was finally in order. And with so much infrastructural decay addressed, there was an opportunity to at last begin talking about more aggressive city building. Or so one might have thought.

III

THE TAXPAYER REVOLUTION AND THE
CITIZEN COUNTER-REVOLUTION

1

On October 25, 2010, Rob Ford was elected to the highest office in Canada's largest city and, to the downtown urbanists who'd functioned as the city's ruling class for most of its post-millennial history, the moment was apocalyptic. He had won in a landslide. His worship, Rob Ford, mayor of Toronto: it was difficult to even fathom.

Yet there he stood on election night, clutching the podium and reading, in halting, stumbling phrases, his address to those he'd been elected to lead. 'Tonight,' he said, 'the people of Toronto are not divided. We are united. We are united, all of us.' Rivers of sweat streamed from the peninsula of his thin, spiky hair, down through the narrows between his sun-bleached eyebrows.

He grinned at the whistles and cheers of the thousands standing before him at the Toronto Congress Centre, some twenty-eight kilometres west of city hall in deep Etobicoke and just a few minutes' drive from the border of the city of Mississauga.

It was a venue in an industrial park in an offstage area of Toronto far from the walkable neighbourhoods and landmark buildings that together add up to the psychological entity of Toronto, its key virtue being access to the highways leading to and from the outer suburbs and the jets above that carry people to other cities around the world. The Toronto Congress Centre is virtually impossible to get to by public transit, and it's in a land where bikes are no more than children's toys. It is no accident that it was here, in the uncelebrated suburban fringe of Toronto, that Ford kicked off his campaign for mayor, and here that he celebrated his victory, under the Uncle Sam–style red, white and blue banners of his campaign, in a room filled with drunken, shouting supporters chanting his name.

One of those supporters interrupted his speech to drape a garish lei around his neck, a floral garland that made it look as though he was embarking on a tropical vacation. Ford continued, enumerating the slogans that had defined his campaign and have since become iron-cast clichés. He was going to 'Stop the Gravy Train' and 'End the War on the Car.' He would slash the office expense accounts of city councillors and take a hard line with the civil-service unions. He would bring 'Respect for Taxpayers' to city hall and eliminate both the vehicle registration and land transfer taxes.

To the so-called 'downtown elites' who opposed Ford, his campaign slogans didn't even cohere into a rational argument. As anyone who followed city hall at all could tell you, the billions of dollars of waste he claimed he could cut simply did not exist. And the combination of massive tax cuts and slashed government spending appeared nonsensical when considered in combination with his insistence – his 'guarantee,' actually – that no city services would be cut, that customer service would be enhanced and that new subways would be built in sparsely populated suburban areas. When you combined these actual platform planks with his off-the-cuff remarks about ripping out streetcars, closing the city's borders to new immigrants and supporting the 'traditional definition' of marriage, and then when you combined *those* statements with his record of being unable to get along with anyone on city council, his tendency toward outbursts of childish, rage-induced ranting in the council chambers and his record of personal problems – when you added all of that up, the election of Rob Ford to the mayor's office looked to a lot of his opponents like a kamikaze vote from people who hated the city.

But to the crowd gathered in the Toronto Congress Centre – and the 47 per cent of voters they represented in the election results – his election was a victory for the underdog. The outright disdain of the political establishment toward Ford represented only an elite who had grown disdainful for what Councillor Mike Del Grande called the 'average Joe,' a composite citizen we can assume suffers from some of the same personal problems Ford does, who's as prone to expressing anger and frustration as he is, who has as little understanding of the nuances of the municipal bureaucracy as he does and, above all, who shares his conviction that no matter how much you want to fancy talk around it, the money of taxpayers is virtually being flushed down the toilet. Retiring councillor Kyle Rae had tried to explain his $12,000 farewell party by talking about the technicalities of campaign surpluses. Ford turned that event into a resonant symbol; it was typical of the city government's wasteful attitude toward taxpayer dollars, and it was disrespectful.

That disrespect was to end. Ford beamed at the people chanting his name. 'This victory is a clear call from taxpayers,' he said. 'Enough is enough, and I want respect.' The assembled masses cheered louder. 'If you voted for me, I thank you from the bottom of my heart. You voted for change and you can trust me to live up to your expectations, guaranteed. Four years from tonight you'll look back and say, "Rob Ford did exactly what he said he was going to do."'

At that moment, I was standing at a much different victory party (in Kensington Market, of course), where the prospect of Ford doing exactly what he said he was going to do was considered a nightmare. Adam Vaughan had been returned to council with a huge mandate, more than doubling the number of votes he'd gotten in the previous election, yet his assembled campaign volunteers and supporters at the Supermarket nightclub were grim. Rob Ford's election as mayor had been declared by the television networks almost as soon as the polls closed, while there were still only three people in the room at Vaughan's party. His volunteers arrived back from a day of pulling the vote to the certain knowledge that though they had won the local battle, and won it convincingly, their side had lost the city-wide war.

Vaughan, a former television broadcaster and second-generation progressive city councillor, had been widely touted as a promising candidate for mayor and was among Ford's fiercest, most articulate critics. At one point Ford demanded that Vaughan 'be a man' and run for the top job; Vaughan demurred, insisting that his constituents in the downtown Ward 20 were his primary concern and that his young children needed his attention. But in many ways Vaughan appeared to be the anti-Ford, slim and silver-haired in his forties, clad in tailored suits and designer glasses, well-spoken and combative and always ready to deliver a long-winded, literate lecture on city-planning theory. He'd been raised at the foot of Jane Jacobs, a family friend and political ally of his father's, and invoked her name at every opportunity. Moreover, he was a champion of smart high-rise development that would allow large families and low-income residents to remain in Toronto's gentrifying downtown, and an advocate of bike lanes and pedestrianism who did not get his driver's licence until he was over forty.

Vaughan's ward represents, in many ways, the neighbourhoods that are central to Toronto: Jacobs' home in the Annex; the city's brain at the University of Toronto; its institutional centre in the hospital corridor on University at the very edge of the financial district; the cultural hub of Queen West; the boho paradise of Kensington Market; the theatre district on King; the breakneck condo-community growth of the waterfront. His ward is home to both the CN Tower and Rogers Centre, seven streetcar routes and two subway lines, as well as the CBC headquarters, the Metro Toronto Convention Centre, the Art Gallery of Ontario and the Royal Ontario Museum. On election night, the residents of this most iconic of Toronto districts returned the anti-Ford to city hall with a 75 per cent supermajority, and voted against Ford on the mayoral ballot by almost the same margin.

And yet here we were at Supermarket, on other nights a venue for book launches and indie-rock dance parties, and the newly elected mayor was on TV talking about how we were united. Onstage with his wife and children, Vaughan said the electorate had sent a message of humility to the city's politicians, urging them to get back to basics, and he said it was incumbent on council to hear that message. But he noted, too, to the delight of the crowd in attendance, that he would not be a yes-man for the new mayor, that the city needed to move forward, to say 'yes' to building the city as well as saying 'no' to things.

After his speech, Vaughan nonetheless told reporters he'd attempt to find common ground with his political rival. The Supermarket crowd was less optimistic about the prospects of harmony. 'These people hate the city,' someone said, gesturing at the TV. 'I can't believe that idiot is our mayor. He's going to destroy Toronto.'

2

Rob Ford was a long shot when he declared his candidacy for mayor – as much so as David Miller had been. Five left-leaning councillors made a thousand-dollar bet with Ford, wagering that, for all his bluster, he wouldn't actually run. Two of the councillors involved told me slightly different versions of the same line: 'It's worth my money to never have to deal with him again on council.' If he ran for mayor and lost, he would no longer be at city hall ranting about penny-ante expenses. But the thought that he might actually win was beyond the realm of imagination. He was a loner on council, an outcast even to the city's established right-wing politicians, with no support from any of the power brokers who help run successful political campaigns.

George Smitherman, the provincial Liberal (and veteran of the Barbara Hall collapse), was a prohibitive favourite. It was thought that the only thing that could keep Smitherman from winning was if John Tory decided to enter the race, but Tory had announced he was staying out and, anyhow, it's not clear their platforms would have differed much. Smitherman positioned himself to run against the Miller administration, painting a picture of fiscal incompetence and waste and promising a form of tough-love management that would bring the unions to heel and be ruthless in making government efficient. Smitherman had attracted the support of the Liberal establishment and the old Lastman-era crony Conservatives alike. In the run-up to the election campaign, someone close to David Miller's office told me privately over drinks that Smitherman's emerging coronation was a message from the backroom boys. 'This is the Family Compact saying, "You've had your fun, but we'll be taking our city back now." Smitherman's not as ideal for them as John Tory would be, but he's made it clear that they can work with him. And so they've turned him into their guy.'

Meanwhile, Karen Stintz, the councillor thought most likely to hold up the right-wing banner in the election, finally announced she wouldn't run, because the fundraisers and organizers she would depend on were waiting around to see if Tory would call on them.

After Miller's surprise announcement that he would not run for a third term, the machinery of his electoral and political success passed over expected candidate Shelley Carroll – Miller's suburban budget chief – and settled first on young, ambitious TTC chair Adam Giambrone. (Late in the campaign, at a barbecue in a Don Mills backyard, Carroll reflected in a conversation with me about how both she and Stintz – two strong women – had been forced from the race because they couldn't draw support from the backroom boys. 'Imagine the debates we could have had,' she said.) After Giambrone flamed out within weeks in a blaze of personal controversy over extramarital – or extra-premarital, since he was not officially married to his partner – sexual shenanigans that apparently extended to the couch in his city hall office, campaign manager John Laschinger and the Miller team moved on to support Joe Pantalone, a council lifer best known as an advocate of the Front Street Extension road expansion. Pantalone's candidacy inspired exactly no one – the press speculated that running was a symbolic retirement gesture from him – but he was left to wave the Miller flag in the face of the oncoming Smitherman juggernaut. Two other no-hope 'front-runners,' Liberal fixer Rocco Rossi and small-time magazine publisher Sarah Thompson, entered the race running to Smitherman's right. (Giorgio Mammoliti was also among the candidates early on – running what appeared to be a kamikaze anti–Rob Ford campaign – until he withdrew in favour of aligning himself with the front-runner and returning to his old council seat.)

When Ford entered the race, in fact, he was heralded only by the talk-radio hosts who had relied on him for easy theatrics and bombast. ('He was the bull in the china shop,' AM640 host John Oakley replied when asked by the *National Post* why he'd made Ford a regular guest. 'The information and the takeaway is just kind of a by-product ... You want to build the biggest audience you can, so your salespeople can take it out to prospective clients, and that's where you create the transaction that makes everybody happy and sustains your living.') But Ford had a simple, strident message that took what the variously conservative candidates running against him – George Smitherman, Rocco Rossi and Sarah Thompson – had defined as the key issue of the campaign (spendthrifts at city hall are out of touch with their constituents and fiscally irresponsible) – and distilled it into an extreme, easy-to-understand message. 'Stop the Gravy Train' meant ending fat union contracts and nickel-and-dime self-dealing through office expenditures. Ford's numbers were very specific: he promised to cut $525,682,075 in waste in his first year in office alone, and $3,018,549,221 over the course of his four-year term. And he guaranteed, as he said repeatedly, that he would not cut services.

His other slogans were equally blunt instruments. 'Respect for Taxpayers' was, above all else, about delivering excellent customer service while slashing tax rates and repealing new taxes that had been imposed by Miller. 'End the War on the Car' was a simple assertion that gridlock was being caused not by suburban sprawl but by bike lanes and streetcars, and a promise to ensure those driving into the city core from the suburbs would find the roads accommodating.

Taken together, these slogans tapped into the alienation of those who felt government was a constant, pernicious imposition on – and certainly no help to – their lives. It helped Ford that he had spent most of his time as councillor acting as a glorified constituency assistant. When Ford's campaign told the press he had banker's boxes containing tens of thousands of phone numbers for voters he'd personally tried to help over the course of his career, reporters thought he was exaggerating. But I had seen with my own eyes how he visited more than a dozen constituents a day. An astounding number of people in Toronto – many of whom had never actually turned out to vote before – felt a connection to Ford that had been forged through personal contact with him. And that kind of contact is powerful. Late in the campaign, Shelley Carroll told me she wasn't sure Ford's lead in the polls at the time would hold up. When she was knocking on doors, the people who told her they were voting for Ford were people she knew hadn't voted in a municipal election in years. On election day, Ford beat Smitherman in Carroll's ward by more than 20 per cent of the vote.

And then there was the matter of Ford's personal behaviour. During the campaign, we could see those lapses were not behind him: on one occasion, Ford commiserated on the phone with an ill man unable to get pain medication – Ford asked the man if he'd tried to 'score it on the street' and then offered to try to buy him some meds on the black market. It turned out the call was being taped and it soon landed in the newspapers. Another lowlight was when a *Toronto Sun* reporter dug up a record of Ford's decade-old arrest in Florida on charges of drunk driving and marijuana possession; Ford denied, then recanted the denial. But such foibles never hurt him, before, during or after the campaign (they continued virtually uninterrupted after his election). As embarrassing and inappropriate as many of Ford's critics believe his behaviour to be, it was not seen as a problem by those who voted for him. Indeed, it might have actually been an asset.

Nick Kouvalis, the campaign strategist who ran Ford's election campaign and later served as his chief of staff, bragged to *Maclean's* magazine that Ford was the first candidate to ever see his poll numbers rise immediately after having his mugshot appear on the front page of the paper. His personal failings enhanced his credibility. A guy that apparently guileless, unhinged and fallible didn't seem capable of the inauthenticity most politicians seem to possess. Analyst Trish Hennessy of the Centre for Policy Alternatives wrote on her blog about a focus group of Ford voters conducted by Environics Research Group, and arrived at this astonishing conclusion: 'When they talked about Rob Ford, they often spoke in appreciative, glowing terms – in the same way they spoke about another well-loved politician, Jack Layton ... They saw little ideological divide between Jack Layton and Rob Ford. Rather, they felt the two men had in common a sincere drive to take on the struggle of the people despite great odds.'

As Ford was exploiting his outsider bona fides, a desperate Smitherman tried to reposition himself closer to the centre of the political spectrum, and then eventually closer to the quasi-Millerian centre-left – highlighting his own status in the gay community and advocating respect for immigrants and the disadvantaged. But like a rerun of the Barbara Hall campaign that Smitherman had co-chaired in 2003, he failed to articulate a clear picture of what he stood for and his vision for the city. He originally defined himself as the anti-government candidate and framed the race as a competition to run vigorously against Miller's record, and then found himself outflanked by three more extreme versions of that position. Rob Ford was the real deal when it came to anti-establishment populist crankiness; for Ford it was not a strategy, it was the very definition of his core principles. And while, in the dying days of the campaign, much of Miller's old constituency flocked to Smitherman's side, Ford creamed him on election day.

3

When Miller hoisted a broom above his head at the Bamboo in 2003, and when Rob Ford had a plastic lei placed around his neck at the Toronto Congress Centre seven years later, both represented enormous grassroots victories. The analysis of what followed doesn't change the lesson both illustrate – that the conventional wisdom of political insiders and pundits can be, and regularly is, thwarted by the people of the city.

But their similarity actually leads to the core philosophical difference between the two: Miller's promise was to enable people to better participate in city government; Ford's was to make city government a better servant to more people. It may seem like a slight distinction, but it speaks volumes. And you could see it most clearly articulated in the language each politician used. Ford, famously, talked endlessly about 'taxpayers.' Miller openly rejected that characterization and preferred to talk about 'citizens.'

Obviously, most voters are both citizens and taxpayers,. (Some of the poor and homeless pay no property taxes, but they all pay sales taxes, at least. And many residents of the city who do pay taxes are not actually Canadian citizens, so they can't vote.) But the contrast in terms is less revealing for the legal or dictionary definitions than for the way they frame the relationship between government and governed. Under the kind of social contract outlined by the great Western philosophers Hobbes, Locke and Rousseau, a citizen enjoys a relationship with government that carries both rights and obligations – there is the implication of participation in elections but also in the smooth functioning and development of society. In ancient Greece, citizenship was highly exclusive but it endowed freedom and privileges while involving active participation in a government assembly. Our concept of citizenship today is far broader – not exclusive to the wealthy or titled – but still involves being endowed with rights by virtue of a relationship with society that also carries certain duties to fellow citizens, both through the state and in private life. We speak of someone volunteering for a charity or helping an old lady across the street as acts of 'good citizenship.' The government is made up of citizens, governs only with the consent of the citizens and involves citizens by allowing and sometimes demanding their participation.

The term *taxpayers*, however, frames the relationship of a person to her government as primarily an economic transaction. One pays taxes to government. What does one get in return? This is a portrayal of the taxpayer as primarily a consumer of government, but even in that it emphasizes a limited part of their consumer relationship. People in this formulation may be voters, they may be users of infrastructure, receivers of grants, visitors to parks, recipients of services. Maybe. But as taxpayers, their important role is in writing cheques. The emphasis on the taxpayer-government relationship focuses on what is taken from citizens rather than on what they receive as a benefit or in what things they are able to participate.

At the Gladstone event during David Miller's 2003 campaign, he addressed this contrast directly. He said it was important that the city's residents be thought of as citizens rather than as taxpayers. Miller spoke about the stirrings of a 'movement' of which he was a part, saying his goal was that after his first term, he wanted people to look back and say, 'Holy shit! We'd forgotten what we could do together as citizens.'

Rob Ford didn't get into any philosophical discussions about his vision of the taxpayer as the most important role in society. But he hammered away at the phrase 'Respect for Taxpayers' during his campaign, and relentlessly asserted that their money was being wasted. If one was in doubt about his concept of citizenship as pure consumerism, it was dispelled by his other emphasis, on 'customer service.' Those two sides of Ford's definition of citizenship, as 'taxpayers' and 'customers,' frames a relationship that's largely passive, and no different from the relationship you have with a corporation – you give them money, they give you goods and services, and their only guarantee to you is that you get what you pay for, and you'll pay as little as you can.

My characterization of those two different terms may make it clear which I think is more appropriate. And that might say something about my political opinions, but it also says something about the place I live, my relationship to my neighbours and the position I occupy in society. A concept of constituents that portrays them as active participants in society and government, I'd suggest, speaks to those who are already actively participating in society and who would like to see their efforts bear more fruit; a call for more participatory democracy will resonate most with those who have been actively trying to participate. Look at me: a journalist living and working mostly in the old City of Toronto through the Miller years, paying close attention to policy and voicing my opinions regularly – already a participant. A concept of my role that portrays me as a partner in the work of building the city is flattering to me, and also fits into my egocentric idea of how the city is progressing.

However, those who feel they are isolated from the larger city they live in, who interact with the public sphere mainly when they write their property tax cheque and when they put their garbage out or wait for a bus or get pulled over by the police – or who at least *perceive* those moments to be the extent of their relationship with government – might think a customer-company analogy is completely appropriate. They might have no reason to believe that people like them will ever be involved in making decisions beyond the ballot box, and they may not even see why they would ever want to. If the neighbourhood you chose to live in largely because it was what you could afford seems to be declining, and if the incomes of the people around you are falling, you might think the city you live in is rigged in favour of others who seem to be getting richer. And if the city services in your area are thin on the ground, parks far away, transit inconvenient and unreliable, you might reasonably think the government is not working for you. If you live in a place like Woburn, where residents say a lack of any sense of 'community' or 'neighbourhood' is one of its defining characteristics, talk of empowering residents to participate might just seem wacky and out of touch.

And if, despite all this, your taxes keep going up? Then the most attractive thing a politician can promise is probably better services and fewer costs, preferably at the same time. That's what you would ask of a company you did business with. To borrow a favourite Ford analogy, if you think of the government as a business, there's a difference in what appeals to people who think of themselves as shareholders in the company, and what appeals to those who think of themselves as customers of the company. We are all both, of course. But a lot of things can influence which side of the transaction you see yourself on most often.

I have a sense of this, because during the 2010 election campaign, by chance, my family moved from Miller Land to Ford Nation. Before the campaign, we lived in an apartment at Dundas and Pacific, in the rapidly gentrifying Junction neighbourhood you always read about in the Style section of the *Globe and Mail*. This is where you'll find Crema Coffee Co., an artisanal café that serves one of the best lattes in the city. Across the street, there's a Starbucks, right next door to a doggy spa. Dundas West and the area around it is the part of the neighbourhood where the Junction Arts Festival is held, the place where all the weekend flâneurs drool over salvaged architectural artifacts at Post and Beam, and where parents wheel their strollers into Vine Avenue Park for singalongs and hot-dog barbecues and buy T-shirts that say 'My Park Is Di-Vine' to raise money to paint the wading pool. My own kids go to school down there, on Annette Street, where they have a French immersion program and the students score well above the provincial average on standardized tests. This part of the Junction is where my family eats brunch on the weekend. It's where we take our one-year-old for playtime. It's where we buy our organic vegetables. Real estate prices here have risen faster than any other in the city, by 44 per cent in the four years before this book was published.

That part of the Junction is in Ward 13 – which has been represented at different times by David Miller, former premier Bob Rae and beloved former mayor David Crombie – and it's where NDP-backed candidate Sarah Doucette beat right-leaning city council incumbent Bill Saundercook in the 2010 election. In addition to the Junction, Ward 13 includes the famously leafy, livable neighbourhoods of High Park, Bloor West Village, Baby Point and Swansea. In Ward 13, Mayor Rob Ford was crushed at the ballot box, earning less than 35 per cent of the vote.

But all that cultural, retail and progressive political life is on the other side of the tracks. Literally. The Junction we live in now – north of the CN Rail underpass, at Keele and Junction Road – is a five-minute walk and an entire world away. It's Rob Ford Country.

When maps showing the distribution of votes for Ford and Smitherman in the election appeared, they confirmed the political and cultural divide between the old, downtown City of Toronto and the former municipalities of York, North York, East York, Scarborough and Etobicoke. The Junction sits right on that now-defunct border. That division was not some new miracle of Rob Ford's populist magic – maps showing the votes for David Miller and John Tory in 2003, or Mel Lastman and Barbara Hall in 1997, look similar, if less starkly pronounced, in their vote distributions. But if I want an illustration of the cultural divide, I don't need to look at a map. I just need to take a walk around my neighbourhood.

From my front lawn, across four lanes of jam-packed, high-speed traffic, I can see a giant warehouse complex where the parking lot is full of tractor trailers and signs advertise vacancies with access to rail. All around, we've got big-box stores, just like in a real suburb: Home Depot, Rona, Canadian Tire, Future Shop, Staples and, beyond them, Walmart, Metro and a TD Canada Trust with a drive-through ATM. There are hectares and hectares of parking lots. Coffee? There's a Country Style with a drive-through. Restaurants? Take your pick: McDonald's, Harvey's, Swiss Chalet, Tim Horton's and a Subway a little farther along.

If you're thinking about buying or fixing a car, there are more than a dozen new and used car lots within walking distance to the north and west, and as many garages. In fact, we share our back lane with a couple of auto mechanics, in addition to an ironworks and a linen-supply company. There's a working rubber factory around the corner. A block and a half northeast of us, near one of the best Italian cheese factories in the city on Mulock Avenue (where people line up for fresh, still-warm ricotta on weekends), we thought we might be getting some new condo towers, but city hall turned down the application because it wanted to preserve the industrial nature of the neighbourhood, and local businesses were worried that an influx of new residents would make the area unfriendly to the heaviest of heavy industry.

There's a parkette across the street from the vacant lot where the condos won't be going, but we don't take our kids there because it's empty and dirty.

This part of the Junction is in Ward 11, home to such unsung neighbourhoods as Rockcliffe-Smythe, Mount Dennis and Weston. Sixty per cent of voters in Ward 11 supported Mayor Rob Ford in the 2010 election, and an even higher percentage of us re-elected right-wing councillor Frances Nunziata, who went on to be the council speaker in Ford's administration.

As a dues-paying member of the so-called downtown Toronto elite who is now resident in Ford Country, I found it particularly interesting to hear my friends raging on about the selfish suburban bigots who elected Ford. There was a feeling that overweight white guys driving expensive SUVs were raining on our Pedestrian Sundays. There seemed, actually, to be some bigotry involved in the caricature of the Ford voter – modelled after the red-faced rage machine himself – that led people to start semi-serious discussions about municipal separatism.

I could go on and on about the anecdotal divisions between Ward 13 (home to High Park and Max's Fine Foods) and Ward 11 (where, on a single block of Eglinton, there are five 'traffic-ticket specialists'). But the distinctions that separate us are more than anecdotal. Though we're neighbours, the progressive wonderland just south of the tracks is whiter, richer and better educated. In Ward 13, the median household income is $61,987, according to the 2006 census, roughly 45 per cent higher than in my new neighbourhood in Ward 11. In Ward 13, only 16.3 per cent of the population are visible minorities, versus 52 per cent in Ward 11. Almost half of Ward 13 residents have a university degree, while only 16.7 of us north of the tracks do.

These are trends that exist city-wide, as I detailed earlier. If you took the election map depicting Ford and Smitherman voters and looked at the demographic data, some pretty stark differences begin to appear – it's the Hulchanski report played out at the ballot box. The median individual income in Ford Country is just under $35,000, while in Smitherman wards it is over $50,000. Households in wards that went to Ford had an average of 1.2 cars each, while Smitherman's wards had fewer than one car per household – and correspondingly, statistics show that the former use transit far less often. The majority (53 per cent) of residents in Ford's wards were visible minorities, while less than 30 per cent of residents in the Smitherman wards were. Voters in the Ford wards were also significantly more likely to have dropped out of high school and less likely to have completed university.

Of course, there are wealthy white people who voted for Ford and poor non-whites who voted for Smitherman. But when you map it, you see something interesting. Rosedale, St. James Town, Cabbagetown and Regent Park – affluent and impoverished neighbourhoods that butt right up against each other in the dense central city – all voted against Ford. Meanwhile, the neighbourhoods that supported Ford, including wealthy ones like the Bridle Path and Royal York, and poor ones such as Malvern and Jane-Finch, are geographically and psychologically isolated from each other – and from the rest of the city. In the dense, transit-heavy neighbourhoods of the downtown core, people voted for progressive candidates. In the sprawling, isolated neighbourhoods of the suburbs, people rich and poor alike chose Ford. Every single polling station in every single priority neighbourhood showed a win for Ford on election day. Three of the four pilot sites for Tower Renewal voted for Ford. Virtually all of Eglinton Avenue, the pending site of Transit City's flagship underground LRT line, voted for Ford. To downtowners, at least, these people seemed to have voted against their own interests.

But why? As a resident of Ford Country with connections to others in Scarborough, Don Mills, Etobicoke and North York, I can hazard a guess. Most of the people who would have been served by those initiatives were unaware they existed, or didn't think they would work. The places they live are geographically isolated from city hall and the seamlessly networked downtown core, and that geography supports an attitude of disengagement. What people up my block and in my parents' neighbourhood share, among other things, is the sense that city hall is a faraway place populated by people unlike them, and that their neighbourhoods have somehow been left out of the discussion. Almost none of the dozen random people at Eglinton and Keele I spoke to one day in the week after the election knew that the proposed LRT line there would run underground, therefore making it a subway in all but name. They had visions of the slow-moving, over-budget, traffic-snarling St. Clair streetcar line dancing in their heads. Rob Ford and his brother Doug constantly underscored this impression during the campaign and after it, promising that Transit City would be just like St. Clair. Simply put, while Miller had attempted to improve the suburbs through many of his showcase policies, the message had not been sufficiently imparted to – or was not appreciated by – the intended beneficiaries.

If you don't have the sense that you are a part of a vibrant community that's getting better and where you and your neighbours are making it better – an impression you might get if you lived near Dufferin Grove Park or Vine Avenue Park south of my house – then what you notice about city politics is what hits you directly: TTC strikes, garbage strikes, new tax notices, snarled traffic, constant construction. And it isn't like people living in the outer city are unaware of how downtown has been developing and succeeding: those who live in Scarborough or Etobicoke often work downtown, travel into the city for hockey games or live theatre, go to the Eaton Centre to shop or to the bars on Queen West to see live bands. And so even if you live in one of the neighbourhoods in the city where everyone seems to be getting poorer and services don't seem to be improving all that quickly, you can still see that for the people in the city who can afford to live right in the heart of it all, everything's getting fancier – new coffee shops and pet salons are serving the shiny new condo towers and the city is installing new bike lanes that make it easier for those living there to get around even as they seem to slow traffic for those who need to commute into the area.

If you are aware of the efforts to make your neighbourhood more like the ones downtown – and you need to be paying close attention to really know about those efforts – you can also see how long that kind of transformation is likely to take. Installing a bike lane on Markham Road is not going to do much to make cycling a viable means of regular transportation out in Woburn. And so maybe there's some chance that in twenty or thirty years your neighbourhood might be more walkable and vibrant and have real rapid transit, but your taxes are going up *today*, and are apparently helping to pay for the renaissance of downtown urbanism. When you do start paying attention come election time, things like $12,000 parties just confirm the gut instinct that the money isn't coming back into your neighbourhood.

It's an uphill battle explaining how building new roads will increase gridlock (since traffic always rises to meet the supply of roads), while getting people on bikes and, especially, onto street-cars will actually decrease congestion. It isn't an intuitive idea. What is intuitive is that the city could save money by getting staff to water their own office plants, as Ford repeated often on the campaign trail.

You could call Rob Ford profoundly uninformed, unpolished, hotheaded and simple-minded – and I think he is all of those things – but those qualities seem unimportant next to the fact that he seems to get it and to genuinely care about the people who are not involved in the urban conversation. In his shaddap-about-nuances rhetoric and his rage at seemingly unnecessary waste, they see their own frustrations reflected, their own impatience with the condescension of a so-called elite. And in that, they see a lot to like.

4

Toward the end of the campaign, I was having a late-night drink with a political insider who had been a key part of the crowd around David Miller's administration. It was not someone I knew particularly well, but it was a drunken after-party kind of conversation, and it was pretty straightforward. Both of us agreed that it was difficult to see how, if Ford was elected, he would actually accomplish anything. His agenda was extreme – far to the right of anything proposed by the likes of John Tory – and in parts transparently unworkable. He had never had any real council allies and had never shown the ability to twist arms or sweet-talk anyone else into agreeing with him. And he had a short temper to boot. He seemed destined to be a one-term mayor, a complete flame-out.

And here's the interesting thing: to the person I was talking to, that scenario seemed preferable to a Smitherman victory. In his eyes, Smitherman looked like a kinder, gentler, slow-motion Rob Ford – he was far slicker and was certain to be more effective at the backroom deals and public diplomacy that would get his agenda implemented. And that agenda, as he had laid it out and the coalition of big-money backers he'd assembled seemed to show, involved cutting city services, playing hardball with unions and keeping taxes down at the expense of infrastructure – all the things Ford was promising but presented with a more moderate, sympathetic face.

As another lefty politico who was there looked on in shock, this guy said, 'If Pantalone doesn't get above 30 per cent in the polls, I'm voting for Rob Ford.' Ford's very extremism and more objectionable qualities would make him easier to rally against and easier to beat. I did not disagree with his logic.

But shortly after the election, it started to look like we might have underestimated the new mayor.

On his first official day in office, Mayor Rob Ford declared Transit City 'dead' and instructed the TTC's general manager to start working on a new plan based around subways. The province, who was paying for Transit City and had already signed contracts for much of the work and begun construction on Sheppard Avenue, announced it was going to renegotiate based on the mayor's wishes. It appeared the mayor was able, suddenly, to govern by fiat, without consulting City Council.

For his first formal City Council meeting, during which he was sworn in as mayor, Ford invited loudmouthed *Hockey Night in Canada* commentator Don Cherry to speak. Cherry took the opportunity to verbally face-wash all the 'left-wing pinkos' who 'ride bicycles and everything.' He said to the mayor's detractors, 'He's gonna be the greatest mayor this city has ever, ever seen, as far as I'm concerned! And put that in your pipe, you left-wing kooks.' So much for the city being united.

At the first working meeting of council, Ford rammed through many of his marquee campaign promises: the Vehicle Registration Tax was eliminated, councillor expense budgets were cut almost in half and TTC workers were declared an essential service, denied the right to strike. The moves were fiscally reckless. Cutting the vehicle tax would cost the city more than $60 million per year in revenue. Because arbitrated contracts almost always give unions a better deal than negotiated ones, some staff and outside analysts – including the right-wing C. D. Howe Institute – estimated the essential-service designation would add about $25 million over three years to the TTC's labour costs (compounded over time with jumps whenever a new contract was signed). As for the expense accounts, Ford's smoking-gun evidence of gravy and waste, reducing those budgets would save the city roughly a million dollars.

Councillors tried to debate him on this, but he refused, politely, to talk about the numbers beyond saying he'd promised to save taxpayers money and cut waste, and that's what he was doing. His supporters on council did not speak about most of the items or engage in any debate – new TTC chair Karen Stintz stayed silent even on the question of declaring public transit workers an essential service – and Ford won pretty much every vote 29–16 or 28–17. This was the pattern for his first six months in office.

He announced – surprise! – that despite his impression that the city was in dire financial straits, he would insist on a property tax freeze in his first budget (since property taxes do not rise with inflation, a freeze is equivalent to a tax cut), that TTC fares would also be frozen and that the writing and passing of the budget would be 'accelerated' – there would be limited debate and no public hearings. Council granted his wishes. He ticked off a list of populist initiatives: contracting out garbage collection in the west end of the city, firing the Toronto Community Housing board after an unfavourable expense report from the auditor general, cancelling construction of a pedestrian bridge near Fort York and removing the bike lanes on Jarvis Street. Almost all of this was stealthily pushed through at the end of meetings and then fast-tracked to avoid any significant public debate. He said the $8 billion in provincial money slated to deliver the four new LRT lines in Transit City would now be spent to bury the entirety of the Eglinton line underground. In addition, he would try to find $4 billion or so from the private sector to extend the Sheppard subway into Scarborough. Ford signed an agreement with the provincial government outlining this change of plans. He did not seek council approval for his new transit measures, although the provincial funding was contingent on eventual council approval.

In those first six months, was Rob Ford winning? On most scorecards, he didn't lose a single round, and his opponents hardly landed a punch. And yet he threw his larger ideological promises – fiscal responsibility, transparency, better customer service – into jeopardy. There was a discernable pattern: first, the mayor made a rash, poorly reasoned statement in the press that nonetheless channelled the public's legitimate anger. He then did an end-run around all the usual procedural checks – public hearings, committee debates – to ram the policy through. Council's left-wing members put up a fight that impressed their base while earning no concessions and looking worse for it to the general public. Then Ford won a landslide victory in the council vote, and his will was done.

With each decision, the city was left worse off – financially and otherwise – than it was before Ford took office. Ford blew through the city's savings – the $367 million surplus from the 2010 budget – while cutting off revenue to the tune of $60 million from the vehicle tax and tens of millions more due to his surprise property tax freeze. And while declaring the TTC an essential service gave frustrated riders the satisfaction of knowing they won't face a strike, it will almost certainly, over time, raise the cost of transit salaries by tens of millions of dollars a year.

Putting it all together, Ford's 2011 budget was higher than Miller's 2010 budget. The projected annual shortfall in the budget when Ford arrived was less than $200 million (when the existing surplus was taken into account), yet Ford worked his magic so six months later we faced a projected deficit of $775 million for 2012. Even with Ford still enjoying a 60 per cent approval rating and winning every vote, it was obvious to many that, since he had so explicitly vowed not to cut services, this would pose an obvious conundrum.

Ford promised fiscal responsibility but was steering the city toward a financial cliff. He promised respect and transparency but governed by fiat. He promised no service cuts and enhanced customer service but was suddenly planning a massive slashing of front-line services. And it was at that point that things started to turn.

5

Here's a Toronto story that shifted the whole political landscape of the city.

Beginning in the morning on July 28, 2011, the longest continuous meeting in the history of Toronto municipal government was held at city hall. By the time it wound down the next morning, tables across the second floor were littered with empty Timbits boxes and coffee cups. The committee room, still packed, as the meeting endured into its twenty-third hour, smelled a bit like a hockey locker room, and the people there displayed the kind of slouched giddiness you'd expect from a game after double overtime.

Ford had been chugging Red Bull at the head of the table where he sat with his executive committee, and now he stood to close the meeting. 'I've been in politics eleven years,' he said to the participants in what was being called a 'citizen filibuster,' 'and this is one of my proudest moments. Whether you agree or disagree, you're here.' It had been an uninterrupted marathon, with some 169 speakers weighing in on proposed cuts to city services. Ford thanked the members of his executive committee who had cross-examined the speakers with him, the other (mostly hostile) city council members in attendance and the people of Toronto who had lobbed insults and criticism at him. 'I respect you for your integrity and for fighting for what you believe in,' he said. 'You pat yourselves on the back because I think we all did a great job and we are going to get this city straightened out.'

There was applause and cheering from the otherwise hostile crowd. It was one of those rare moments in the life of the Ford administration (then just over seven tumultuous months old) when all parties, left, right and otherwise, seemed to agree on something. Look at all this democracy, everyone kept saying.

Ford had put the whole thing in motion months earlier when he commissioned the consulting firm KPMG to undertake a broad but cursory investigation of every service Toronto's government offered, with notes about which programs might be expendable. The mayor was trying to thread a very tiny needle here: he had campaigned loudly on slashing government spending and waste, promising billions in savings for taxpayers, to be returned to them in tax cuts. But he had been equally insistent in his campaign that the cheaper government could still do all the same things it had done before. The magic word in Rob Ford's vocabulary was *efficiencies.* And yet when KPMG issued its report, it made no note of possible ways to make service delivery more efficient – studying operations was not part of its assignment. Instead, it put an X through a wide range of services that were not absolutely essential, suggesting they be considered for demolition. Among the proposed cuts in their report, the city could stop fluoridating the water; it could reduce library hours and close some branches; it could decrease the level of snow removal; and eliminate community grants and funding for Business Improvement Area associations.

At Ford's request, KPMG had essentially proposed a whack of service cuts. The mayor gamely denied this was the case, again calling for 'efficiencies.' But the people of Toronto disagreed with Ford's eccentric semantics, and as KPMG's proposals were rolled out gradually, dominating headlines every day for weeks, they were received like a series of punches in the gut. Closing libraries? Cutting jobs in the police department? (Ford campaigned on hiring 500 *more* officers!) Eliminating snow removal on side streets? (*Snow removal?* In Canada? In a city as gridlocked as Toronto?) But here's the punchline: KPMG estimated that if the city implemented every single one of the possible cuts it discussed, the city's budget would shrink by only $100 to $150 million per year, equivalent to about 1 per cent of the budget. As a point of comparison, the tax cuts and freezes Ford had implemented to start the year cost the city about $100 million in annual revenue.

Centrist city councillors, whose votes Ford depended on to govern, and who until then had been reliably, if meekly, taking his side – started responding to constituent outrage, saying publicly they were uncomfortable with the proposals. Even staunch Ford allies such as James Pasternak and Karen Stintz, who had each voted with the mayor 100 per cent of the time, announced they would not support the closing of any library branches.

But, of course, the fight was not just about libraries. Instead, the KPMG report made it about pretty much everything; the massive breadth of the proposals alerted almost every constituency that their own sacred cattle were being led to the slaughter. This was not like contracting out garbage collection, which had outraged labour unions, or removing the recently installed bike lanes on Jarvis Street, which pissed off a very vocal but very narrow constituency of cyclists. This wasn't even like the mayor's stubborn refusal to support the Gay Pride celebrations, which polls showed reflected poorly on him but still might be seen as a niche issue.

By looking at every goddamn thing that was not nailed down, the Core Service Review made the conversation about every goddamn thing at once. Which means the heritage preservation folks and the AIDS program supporters, the library users and the dental health advocates, the labour unionists and the people who own small businesses, all kinds of people who are not typically on the same side of things suddenly found themselves rowing a single boat against the cost-cutting tide.

Ford went on TV a week before the executive committee meeting to dismiss the fuss – it's just efficiencies, he said again – and invited everyone to come on down to city hall to meet each other. 'I'm inviting the whole city,' he said to Stephen LeDrew of CP24. 'I don't care if we have to sit there for three days. Come and let me know what you think we're doing right, what we're doing wrong, and share your ideas. I'm interested in hearing from the taxpayers.'

Come, Rob Ford said, and so they did. More than twenty-eight dozen people signed up to speak, and more people than that crowded into the second floor of city hall, in Committee Room 1, where the committee was gathering, and into Committee Room 2, where a live feed of proceedings was being broadcast for the overflow crowd, and into Committee Room 3, where another live feed was onscreen and a potluck buffet appeared on side tables filled with pots of chili, boxes of pizza and doughnuts, and urns filled with gallons and gallons of coffee. Senior citizens, high school students, business owners, artists, doctors: they waited around for hour upon hour, listening to each other's three-minute sermons on civics and waiting for their own turn at the mic.

I've spent more of my life than I'd like to have sitting through meetings at city hall, and I can say the speeches from the citizens that night were substantially more interesting, and somewhat more succinct, than the standard speeches of the politicians who work there. There was a puppet show, a few poems, a spirited rendition of a Toronto political show tune, the requisite quotations from Oliver Wendell Holmes ('I like taxes, they buy me civilization'), Winston Churchill (on the suggestion that arts funding be cut to fund the war effort: 'Then what are we fighting for?') and Peter Ustinov ('Toronto is like New York run by the Swiss'). There were readings from books by Margaret Atwood and Dr. Seuss.

The über-activist Dave Meslin had drawn a lot of scorn from anti-Fordists like *NOW* magazine because he'd publicly said he would try to work productively with the mayor. But here he stood up and shouted, stabbing his finger in the air, 'As a person dedicated to consultation, I don't think the previous administration was perfect. I expected you might do better, and you've done much worse. And that is shameful.' Former mayoral candidate

Himy Syed gave an impromptu comic masterpiece of a speech full of very specific and apparently workable budget solutions, tailored to each councillor on the committee.

But the moment that was later memorialized in news reports and in blog posts occurred at two o'clock in the morning. A very nervous fourteen-year-old, Anika Tabovaradan, spoke against the library closures. She explained how she needed the computers at Woodside Square library in north Scarborough for her homework, and that there were already long waits. How she often had to sit on the floor because all the chairs were already taken. She spoke haltingly, choking on her tears. 'I hate public speaking,' she gasped. 'But this branch is so important to me ... I'm no taxpayer, but when I get to use the computers in the library and do my homework, I'll be able to get a good job someday, get some good education. And when I can pay taxes I'll be glad that one day years before people paid extra taxes to keep the system going.' The crowd cheered, applauded. I looked beside me in the press gallery, where grown men and women were weeping.

And it went on: don't cut libraries, they said. Don't cut grants, they said. Don't outsource parks maintenance or TTC service or school breakfast programs, they said. When councillor Mammoliti, the former Ford opponent who had by then assumed a role as the unbridled id of the administration, jeeringly asked each speaker where they lived (he assumed they must live downtown) and what solutions they'd offer to the city's budget riddles, they said over and over that the city should raise taxes if it needed to, and look harder for ways to find revenue. At the beginning of the meeting, Ford had said the review was about looking at which things in the city were 'need-to-haves' and which were 'nice-to-haves.' He pointed to a budget gap he then claimed was $775 million and said, effectively, this is why we can't have nice things. To which one of the speakers said, 'What everyone has been saying is that the "nice-to-haves" are the things that make the city worth living in.'

For all the anger and pleading directed at the executive committee throughout the night, there was also a sense of gratitude. Because people who cared so much about whatever they were speaking to had sacrificed a day's work and night's sleep to say it, and they found at city hall an army of fellow citizens just as concerned, perplexed and suddenly motivated as they were. In the two overflow rooms, people were talking, rehearsing their speeches in front of each other and sharing complaints. They gathered their chairs into semicircles and plotted strategy. They exchanged phone numbers and email addresses and resolved to work together.

'Have you been in there?' my friend and former *Eye Weekly* colleague Councillor Gord Perks said to me, pointing at one of the overflow rooms and grinning. I had been speaking with him a lot in the previous months when he was losing every vote to the Ford steamroller. It was nice to see him smile. 'It's like a civics workshop. In two decades of activism – when I was with Greenpeace, the Toronto Environmental Alliance, here – I have never seen public participation like this. This is what I've been waiting for. People are talking to each other about the kind of city they want. It's amazing.'

But when the meeting ended, it ended with a whimper. The executive committee voted to essentially ignore the deputations they'd heard and send all of the KPMG suggestions to the city manager for review. In the hallway, Mammoliti revelled in his role as a straight-talking killjoy, telling any reporters who would listen that they had just heard from the 'usual suspects,' the same band of professional protesters and paid union stooges from downtown who come out to whine at every council meeting. Already in the mumbled conversation of those milling about, and on Twitter, I could hear the giddiness of the sleepover high giving way to frustration. People were saying that the whole thing had been useless, a show trial with a foregone conclusion. The Ford juggernaut was going to roll over these people just as it had rolled over all the other opposition so far.

I smelled like coffee, cigarettes and sweat. Sluggishly, almost in slow motion, I emerged into the sunshine of Nathan Phillips Square, where bright-eyed people in skirts and suits were hustling across the concrete expanse to work, and slouched through the Financial District in a kind of exhaustion-induced intoxication.

The phone in my pocket buzzed several times a minute as people just waking up and checking into their Twitter accounts responded to the reports I'd posted throughout the night. The cranes south of Lake Shore Boulevard added storeys to the growing cluster of glass skyscrapers as those living in the still-new buildings around them awoke; workers on dangling platforms ascended the outside of the Bank of Montreal tower at First Canadian Place to replace the marble that represented 1980s opulence with something more becoming of a global banking giant of the new millennium; excavators at Union Station dug out whole new pathways from beneath the railway tracks even as hundreds of thousands of people roared into the city upon them and then jostled out onto the sidewalk. I was taken by the tidy, obvious metaphor: it was a new day in Toronto, the end of a long, dark night that had given way to a morning shining with new possibilities. For the first time in a long time, Toronto's prospects again struck me as unlimited.

'It's hard to predict anything in politics,' I wrote in a story that would run on the cover of that week's issue of *The Grid*, 'but if at the end of this year, or a year from now, the mayor is fighting for his political life, July 2011 may just have been the point at which the tide turned against him.'

6

For a long time, the Sideshow Rob Extravaganza didn't seem to hurt his public support. But if the massive and nonsensical nature of his policies raised the stakes for those who felt the mayor risked destroying the city, his gaffe-prone persona has made the whole thing fabulously entertaining. The mayor has provided ample, routine opportunities for mockery and self-righteous outrage, and a community of people has engaged in both as a regular pastime.

You can see the effect in the council chamber, where suddenly every meeting features a gallery full of new enthusiasts, almost all of them dead set against Ford's agenda, watching and discussing even the most mundane business. In the Miller years you might have seen fifteen or twenty observers; in the Ford era, the gallery is regularly occupied by more than a hundred. When big issues are up for debate, the room overflows and people watch on television screens in the rotunda downstairs.

Activists started fighting the mayor more directly: Adam Chaleff-Freudenthaler, a former youth activist, member of the library board and failed candidate for school-board trustee, filed a campaign finance audit request that would investigate apparent violations of the law and, if successful, could see the mayor punished or removed from office. When Doug Ford saw Chaleff-Freudenthaler at city hall and warned him, 'What goes around comes around,' the activist filed another complaint with the integrity commissioner that saw the mayoral brother-in-chief forced to apologize. Jude MacDonald, a founder of the left-leaning website Rabble.ca, filed multiple complaints with the city's integrity commissioner over Ford's office expenses and use of his office resources to support his volunteer football coaching. Complaints from unnamed citizens about the civic appointments process led the city ombudsman to conclude that Ford's office had compromised the integrity of the appointments process. The endless complaints were a result of the invigorated opposition to Ford, and news of them just served to further ramp up interest in the gong show.

I can feel the effects of this in my own career: before, my regular readership consisted largely of insiders at city hall and political activists. Since Ford was elected, tens of thousands of readers click through online to soak up anything I write about the mayor; the gas station attendant who sells me cigarettes recognized me from my column photo and now talks to me regularly about municipal affairs; suddenly national entertainment and media celebrities are reaching out to talk about Ford. On Twitter, a few thousand regular users dissect every council decision, and the social-media conversation really comes alive when the mayor does something demonstrably wrong – like giving the finger, allegedly, to a mother who scolded him for talking on his cell while driving. New political micro-celebrities – like Jonathan Goldsbie, the wonky leftist activist, and Matt Elliot, who runs a chart-heavy blog called *Ford for Toronto* – have emerged as their online punditry grows more popular than many newspaper columns. Many others – tweeters with handles like @neville_park, @madhatressTO, @cityslikr and @sol_chrom – were rounded up and nicknamed 'the Scoobies' in a column about their influence by the *Globe*'s Marcus Gee.

This online opposition began discussing how to actively mobilize against Ford's administration, and in August 2011, about two months after the sleepover public meeting at city hall, they were presented with a key opportunity. Councillor Doug Ford appeared on the CBC radio program *Metro Morning* to unveil a vision for fast-tracked development of the Eastern Port Lands, the waterfront industrial district that represented the largest parcel of undeveloped land in the city, directly adjacent to the downtown core. An existing plan, he said, would be thrown out – too slow, he said, and too expensive – in favour of a proposal that included a giant Ferris wheel, a destination megamall and a hotel. The whole thing would be served by a monorail. The news was a surprise to the rest of city council, to the Waterfront Toronto organization that had long been working on the Port Lands and to the people of the city.

But things had changed. This wasn't Transit City – the Fords could no longer simply undo years of work in favour of a halfbaked scheme concocted in some backroom. Waterfront activists and local residents who had been involved in the planning for the Port Lands immediately began organizing, and soon found themselves working in close coordination with social-media regulars. An urban planner and popular tweeter named Laurence Lui met up with the activists and started tweeting about the issue under the Twitter hashtag #CodeBlueTO. He set up a website, while activist and Jude Macdonald set up a Facebook group. Coordinating together mostly online – and meeting up in person twice – the Code Blue group gained 7,000 petition signatures in just three weeks and organized meetings with flexible city councillors (who, in turn, persuaded other potential swing votes). Meanwhile, nearly 151 planning experts wrote a stinging open letter opposing Ford's plan. John Tory's CivicAction group spoke out against it. Less than a month after Doug Ford had announced his new vision for the waterfront, city council definitively killed it in a unanimous vote as the Ford team agreed to a compromise that looked a lot like total surrender.

That turned out to be just a warm-up. In January, the budget – which had been the subject of that overnight meeting – came to city council for a vote. In the face of opposition from within his own inner circle, the mayor first watered things down: trial balloons about closing library branches, for example, got deflated and tossed; the budget committee itself saved school-nutrition programs and backed away from, among other things, closing some community centres and swimming pools. But even with that fiscal dilution, Ford still lost the vote. A majority of councillors revised the budget further to direct $20 million back into the TTC, libraries, environmental programs and community centres.

A sense of inevitability colours that result now, but until then, this city council had never defied Mayor Ford. Unlike with the waterfront, where he quickly backed down, this time Ford fought hard. But the centrists on council who had previously voted with Ford, and even some formerly loyal supporters, voted against the mayor in response to an overwhelming outcry from their constituents. The lesson was clear: council ruled the city, not the mayor, and council took its cues from the voters. The city is bigger than its mayor, and bigger even than city council: citizens showed, as they have throughout the city's history, that you can fight city hall. That if the people of Toronto speak loudly and clearly enough, they can undo the most entrenched plans of the elites. It's how democracy is supposed to work, and how it's always served Toronto. Politically, it represented a thundering defeat for the mayor – a vote of non-confidence in his government, really – and a recalibration of the governing math at city hall. Policy-wise, it represented a shift in momentum, a slowing down of the childish, intentional crapification of the city, hinting perhaps at a deliberate turn toward city building.

The second week of February 2012 was the most significant one at city hall since amalgamation. It began as the week that the city's largest labour union, CUPE Local 416, was wrestled into submission by a bullying administration. And then it became the week that the mayor's administration effectively ended.

On Super Bowl Sunday, Ford's very favourite day of the year, the mayor announced the first good news he'd had in quite a few months: in a miracle on the order of a Manning-to-Tyree late-game bomb, the city had drawn major concessions from the outside workers' union (including garbage collectors) and a deal had been reached to avoid a work stoppage that had come to seem inevitable. In an attempt to live to fight another day, the union essentially folded in the face of Ford's hardball tactics. But the details of that agreement were still being sorted out when the latest edition in a months-long series of Completely Unprecedented Biggest Meetings Ever took place on Wednesday, February 8.

For the first time in the megacity's history, a meeting had been called by city council over the objections of the mayor. And that meeting, initiated by the mayor's own TTC chair, Karen Stintz, was called for the sole purpose of overturning Ford's plan for transit – the largest, most expensive and arguably most important file in the city – and implementing a completely different scheme. Stintz had remained loyal to the mayor even throughout the budget fight, but finally she went public to say that Ford would not listen to reason about transit. It was clear his plan was going to provide far less service at far greater cost. Journalist John Lorinc suggested it would be 'the single most expensive infrastructure mistake in Toronto history.'

When, just as they had a month earlier in rewriting his budget, city council overruled the mayor and implemented a plan identical to Miller's previous Transit City plan, Ford threw a hissy fit. He declared the council vote 'irrelevant.' He said that Premier Dalton McGuinty would disregard the vote – a statement contradicted less than an hour later by the premier, who made it clear he'd already told Ford he would listen to council. And then, rather than regrouping to negotiate with council's centre on how he might regain confidence and implement his own agenda going forward, he went on a midnight TTC ride in Scarborough, commiserating with random riders about how city hall is a hell-hole of waste and disrespect.

That sequence of actions explains a lot – good, bad and ugly – about Rob Ford. Ever since he entered politics, he's held government in general, and city government in particular, in contempt. The kitchen-table wisdom he's loudly proclaimed has been in stark contrast to observable reality. And he has always – *always* – preferred to go out into the street and meet with people to share complaints with them about the city's government than attempt to govern.

Connecting with people in person is Ford's only political skill. And that strength served him well in the past, helping him get elected thrice as a councillor and win the mayoralty. But getting votes is only one-third of a politician's job. Another third is reconciling your policy proscriptions with reality, making sure that what sounded good on the stump will actually work to make the city better. And the remainder of the job is getting stuff done: doing the diplomacy, negotiation and persuasion necessary to win the support of those you need to implement your vision. On both the latter two responsibilities, Ford has consistently failed, and seemed almost constitutionally incapable of reversing course.

A wise politician would have looked down into his hands after the transit meeting, seen that he was holding his own ass and begun reconciling with the key members of council who handed it to him. Instead, Rob and Doug Ford went about immediately setting fire to the few remaining bridges that would allow them to travel back toward relevance and influence. They called Stintz a 'backstabber.' They accused Gordon Chong, their own subway advisor, of proposing 'just another tax grab' for suggesting ways to raise the astronomical funds needed to consider subway expansion. They managed to fire Gary Webster, the manager of the TTC who had made clear his preference for LRT technology, but days later they saw council remove the Ford-friendly councillors on the transit commission and replace them with leftists and Stintz allies.

The news just got worse for the mayor. A new poll showed his approval rating had plunged. The first noticeable result of his budget cuts appeared in the form of a likely $100 increase in registration fees for every child joining a summer baseball or soccer league, a predictable result of new user fees that seemed to take Team Ford off guard (and that council promptly reversed once it became apparent). Even his 'Cut the Waist' weight-loss stunt – in which he weighed himself before a rapt press gallery once a week – stalled, becoming a constant source of animosity between himself, his brother and the media.

That last one, of course, was a purely personal setback, reflecting only Ford's failure to fulfill his own proclaimed goals for his physical fitness. But here's the thing: the entirety of Ford's mayoralty leads to the inevitable conclusion that where he is concerned, the personal is political. The constant sideshow aspects of his political career – drunkenly berating hockey game attendees, offering to score drugs for a voter, etc. – are simply inseparable from the policy and political spheres of his career.

And finally, in September 2012, the collision of his personal failings and his political persona threatened to end his career as mayor.

7

Even his supporters would agree that Rob Ford is not a deep thinker, and he's got a temperament that lends itself to outrageous outbursts and errors in judgment. He means well, I think, almost all the time. But he has a combination of qualities that make him a bit of a public-relations time bomb.

I wouldn't accuse him of having anything like an ideology. He can sometimes look like a libertarian or a corporatist, but he does not cohere to the logical elements of those schools of thought. He starts from two, sometimes contradictory, premises: 1) No taxes are good taxes, and 2) The role of government is to give people what they want directly. As a corollary, he has complete faith in the 'private sector' to deliver anything that is needed, though he does not appear to understand market incentives or how the prospect of profit is necessary to motivate the private sector. This is how he can spend most of his time as mayor, reportedly, visiting tenants in affordable housing to commiserate with them about the crumbling state of their homes and then oppose any spending to address that crumbling infra-structure. He is enraged by 'waste,' but labels 'waste' public funding for anything he doesn't understand – community economic development, health programs or office staff, for exam-ple. He can say in one breath that his own football program, run in a publicly funded school with charitable contributions from him and other corporate donors, is the best anti-gang program, that without it his players would be in jail. And then oppose not just spending money on community sports grants but accepting money from the federal government to support those programs, dismissing them as 'hug-a-thug' enterprises that do not work and are a waste of taxpayer dollars. This is how he can insist that a subway extension into Scarborough expected to cost $2.8 billion or more is his priority, but then not put a single cent of tax money into it. His logic is simple: the people of Scarborough would prefer a subway to any other kind of transit. But he is opposed to spending billions of dollars of tax money, on principle. Therefore, the private sector will pay for it. It is not an argument so much as a wish.

And this is the same logic process – my wish is my command – that led him to repeatedly violate council's ethics guidelines. When he has been found by the integrity commissioner to have improperly used his office in a way that could look like influence peddling – as a mayor and as a councillor – in soliciting donations for the youth sports charity he runs, he has repeatedly defended himself by saying the charity is a good cause. As if that changed what donors who relied on the city for business might expect in return for a donation. And when, as a result of his refusal to personally repay those donations to lobbyists, as he'd been ordered to do by a vote of city council, council held another vote to consider excusing him of the fines, he made an impassioned speech and voted to absolve himself. Voting when you have a financial interest at stake is as clear as conflicts of interest get.

This case arose from a seemingly small conflict, which itself arose from a seemingly small, perhaps understandable ethical issue, surrounding Ford's charity-fundraising tactics. As a coun-cillor, Ford had been using his city hall office stationery and one of his staff members to help run his youth football foundation, drawing donations from eleven companies who lobby for city business. Though it was for a good cause, the integrity commissioner said it was against the rules, and suggested as a punishment that Ford personally repay $3,150 in donations back to the lobbyists. While he was still a councillor, council approved of this penalty and ordered Ford to pay. Once he was mayor, the integrity commissioner came back to council to report that he still had not paid. In February 2012, Ford made a speech saying he shouldn't have to pay and then voted with a council majority to excuse himself from the penalty. The Municipal Conflict of Interest Act clearly says that members of council should not speak or vote on matters in which they have a direct financial interest. Since this vote made Ford $3,150 richer, the conflict seemed clear.

To hold him to account, one private citizen, a business owner named Paul Magder – whose disregard for Ford was apparent, and who had previously filed complaints about his election financing – finally began court proceedings against him. (Magder had apparently been recruited for the task by multiple complainant and labour-relations officer Adam Chaleff-Freudenthaler, who also helped arrange for lawyer Clayton Ruby to represent Magder pro bono.) But even as a judge was deliberating on that complaint, other instances of Ford's reckless disregard for the rules emerged. It appeared he had been using his office staff and resources to help with his football coaching – indeed, one assistant in the mayor's office was the former quarterback of the University of Toronto football team and was always present at practices. It was reported that helping coach the football team, driving players and equipment around in a city-owned car, was the primary job of at least one mayor's-office staffer. Even as the controversy swirled, Ford continued to duck out of important city council meetings for hours at a time to run practices. He called the process of extracting community benefits from developers through Section 37 of the Planning Act a 'shakedown,' yet it was reported he'd had a developer pay Section 37 funds to refurbish the dressing room of his football team. And in a refreshingly un-football-related development, he met with department managers and the deputy city manager personally to fast-track roadwork and landscaping around the property of his family business in time for the company's 50th-anniversary celebrations. But by the time those allegations emerged, he'd already made it pretty clear, in court, that he didn't understand where the ethical boundaries were.

Watching Ford testify at Ontario Superior Court in early September 2012, at the hearing into the civil conflict-of-interest complaint launched by Magder, was supremely uncomfortable. He slouched in the stand next to Justice Charles Hackland in a blue suit, red-faced and pouting, his voice a fragile croak. The expansive mayor of Canada's largest city appeared to shrink throughout the day, as two of the most famous and accomplished lawyers in Canada, Clayton Ruby and Alan Lenczner, argued his fate in terms he frequently claimed he did not understand.

Ruby, acting for the complainant against Ford, reminded him of the oath of office he had sworn four times in ten years, solemnly promising to uphold the Municipal Conflict of Interest Act. 'What steps, if any, did you take to find out what the Municipal Conflict of Interest Act required of you?'

'None,' Ford said softly. There was then a long pause. Four, five seconds? The silence seemed to stretch on.

'None?' Ruby said. Another pause. 'That's your answer?'

'Yes.'

Ruby reminded him that the oath of office he swore as both councillor and mayor specifically contained a promise to uphold the Municipal Conflict of Interest Act, and that the council handbook he would have been given every single time he was elected contained information about the act, and about how to avoid conflicts of interest. Ford said he didn't recall ever getting or seeing or reading a copy. Ruby reminded him of the councillor-orientation sessions available to help teach councillors the basics of the job – sessions that might have covered the act. Ford said that since his father had been a member of provincial parliament, he had not needed to go to any orientation.

Had he ever asked for the free legal advice he was entitled to about conflicts? Or any legal advice? 'I did not.'

Ford had outlined, and would repeatedly outline, his own understanding of the Conflict of Interest Act – 'How I define a conflict of interest is if it's financially beneficial to the city and financially beneficial to me personally.' Therefore, since the actions he was here to defend or explain, speaking and voting on a motion pertaining to whether he should be forced to pay a $3,150 penalty imposed on him by the integrity commissioner, had no financial implication for the city, they were not a conflict. 'Because it doesn't benefit the city. It has nothing to do with the city. This is my issue personally.' Ford insisted he had held this interpretation for twelve years, and moreover he insisted that this was the correct definition.

Ruby had Ford read the relevant passage of the act aloud in court. 'It says nothing whatsoever about the city having a financial interest,' Ruby suggested, and Ford appeared to acknowledge that this was the case.

'I've never read it before,' Ford said.

'You *have* to have read it before! It's the Municipal Conflict of Interest Act!'

'I've never read it.'

'I read it to you at the deposition,' Ruby reminded him, as he started to leaf through his paperwork to find the relevant page of the transcript of that conversation from earlier this summer.

'You read it to me. I've never read it,' Ford said.

A minute later, Ford repeated his understanding of the act's contents. 'I always thought, for twelve years, and I still believe, that a conflict is when the city has a benefit and when I have a benefit. This is a personal issue and had nothing to do with the city.'

A little later, trying to show that Ford's claim to always have believed his benefit-the-city/benefit-me understanding of the matter was disingenuous, Ruby played a video of Ford declaring a conflict of interest on another occasion. At that time, the matter was a report from the integrity commissioner suggesting Ford be reprimanded for an entirely different issue. There were, as laid out in the report, no financial implications from the City at all. Ford, on the video, stood at city hall and said that since the report was about him, he could not speak or vote on it, and he had to leave the chamber. He said it himself, simply and straightforwardly.

'On that day, you understood the simple principle: if the report is about Rob Ford, you can't take part in the debate, yes?' Ruby asked.

'No,' Ford said.

'I heard your voice. I heard you *speak the words*,' Ruby said. 'Did you understand the words as you were speaking?'

'No,' Ford said.

And that sums up the gist of Ford's bewildering testimony that day. He did not seem aware of what a conflict of interest was, or adhered to a definition that conveniently let him off the hook. When confronted with inconsistencies in his own testimony, he shrugged and repeated his understanding of the conflict-of-interest laws, or claimed he couldn't recall, or that he saw no inconsistency.

Anyone with even a fleck of empathy in their heart felt humiliated on behalf of the mayor. I repeatedly felt the urge to translate the proceedings for him. It was not a feeling that the mayor was being treated unfairly, exactly, just a natural reaction to watching him being so thoroughly exposed. Another observer, a woman I met in the elevator, compared the experience to watching a caged animal being repeatedly stabbed with a stick, unable to escape or respond or even understand exactly what was going on.

But at the same time, there was the perhaps more sickening realization that, however uncomfortable it was watching the mayor be subjected to this, he *was* the mayor. And the fact that he seemed unequipped to understand even the simplest levels of abstraction, to comprehend even the simplest pieces of terminology, to even try to learn anything about the procedures of city hall or the law or even to have prepared in any basic way for the questioning he was now undergoing was a shock to the system.

The mayor's own admission, to summarize the gruelling hours of testimony, was that he was – *is* – not just ignorant, but proudly so. That he will proceed, confidently and consistently, from a complete lack of any useful information and refuse to seek any insight or advice that will help dispel his ignorance or clarify his understanding. And that he will do so in the proud, unshakable certainty that he is correct. It wasn't just a lack of expertise or even basic knowledge the mayor displayed, but an outright disdain for expertise and knowledge, coupled with an inability to even understand that this was the case. This was not built into the complaint against him or into Ruby's submission. Ruby's claim, actually, was that the mayor was being dishonest. It was the mayor's own defence that he was not dishonest, but that he was belligerently ignorant: uninformed, unadvised, unwilling to even momentarily consider that his interpretation of things – matters he openly acknowledged he knew nothing about – were in error.

The ethical principles involved in this case – conflict of interest and influence peddling – are important. But the complaint here also deals with cases where the harm is small and, at least in the case of Ford's fundraising, it's easy to see how he could make a mistake until it was brought to his attention. In any event, it seems like the kind of case that might be dealt with by a firm slap on the wrist, perhaps a fine. But the law does not allow for slaps on the wrist; the options are, essentially, no punishment at all or removal from office. If Ford was found to have violated the act, he'd automatically be removed from office unless he could show that he made a legitimate error in judgment or that the amount involved was inconsequential. Which kind of changed the view of the proceedings. There was some angry debate back and forth before the hearing. Ford supporters said it was irresponsible for his opponents to bring down the hammer over such a trivial issue (and besides, think of the youth who benefit from his football program!) and his critics thought the mayor needed to be called to account for his disregard for ethical principles (even though most that it was unfortunate that such a seemingly disproportionate penalty applied).

I think most of us assumed he'd get out of it somehow – he'd say he was sorry, and that he misunderstood but has now changed his ways, or something. What we didn't expect was for the mayor himself to turn it into a hearing about his own basic competency for office, and the competency – by incredibly uncomfortable implicit extension – of the city that elected him.

In Ruby's final submissions, he walked us through Ford's repeated insistence that he had never read the Municipal Conflict of Interest Act or any of the many guides he'd been provided with explaining how to comply with the act, had never sought legal advice on conflicts, had no procedure in his office for trying to identify and avoid conflicts, and had at least once disregarded a friendly heads-up from a political opponent that he might be in conflict. 'That is not good faith,' Ruby said. 'That is wilful ignorance.' He went on, a little later, to say, 'He is clearly not doing what any reasonable person would do. He is proceeding from reckless ignorance.'

Ford sat, frowning, a few feet away. He did not visibly react to any of this. But it wasn't apparent he even would, if inclined to display an emotion other than pouty boredom, react in the way you'd expect of someone accused of being 'recklessly ignorant.' Because here's the thing: *Reckless ignorance was the gist of his own defence testimony*. Ruby suggested he was lying and Ford countering by saying that he was not lying, that he was just proudly ignorant – and believed he was in the right, besides.

And this encapsulated Ford's entire mayoral career. He claimed he could eliminate literally billions of dollars in waste – he 'guaranteed it.' He claimed that proposals to eliminate grants and slash funding for services and, for example, end snow removal on side streets were not 'cuts' but 'efficiencies.' On virtually every issue, this kind of thing. Wilful ignorance. Reckless indifference. He did not understand the words as he was speaking them. He had never tried to. And does not want to. This defence was far more devastating to sit through than any attack on him by an opponent.

And even after it was all over, the legal problems continued to pile up. For a week in November, Ford was in court facing a $6 million libel trial over allegations of corruption he'd made on the campaign trail. At the same time, the results of the audit of his campaign finances was expected shortly. The city hall press gallery seemed to be spending as much time covering court proceedings (and high school football games) as they did writing about city council.

On Sunday, November 25, the Toronto Argonauts won an upset victory in the Grey Cup, held downtown at the Rogers Centre. For a city that has often, in recent decades, simultaneously failed to win major sports championships and forgotten it even has a football team, it was a mildly joyous moment – Toronto seemed pleasantly surprised, more amused than ecstatic. Our football-fan-in-chief, however, was clearly overjoyed. Ford spent the weekend tub-thumping for the Argos and the night of the game screaming himself hoarse cheering them on.

He would still be hoarse the next day, as the press lined up at the University Avenue courthouse to await the judgment on the conflict-of-interest case. I arrived a few minutes before it was to be delivered and found myself near the end of a queue that was more than a hundred journalists long. The judge's decision was being faxed in, and then a clerk needed to make photocopies of it to be handed out, so the wait stretched on until after ten-thirty. In line, reporters cracked jokes about the old-fashioned technology involved – scrolls and stone tablets were invoked – and anxiously checked Twitter to see if, somehow, the decision had leaked.

Finally the giant stack of copies arrived, and the joking stopped as we all filed quickly past the table to grab the decision. As soon as I picked it up, I began flipping through the last pages as I walked, and then saw it in plain type:

[61] Accordingly, I declare the seat of the respondent, Robert Ford, on Toronto City Council, vacant.

Holy shit. Rob Ford was losing his job. This was news I had half-expected, and still it was a shock.

I began tweeting the news, typing into my smart phone as I walked and read. Hackland had suspended the ruling for two weeks to give council time to adjust, and had declined to bar Ford from running for office 'beyond the current term' – a point that led to immediate confusion about whether that meant he could run again for another term if a by-election was called or would have to wait out the end of the current council term in 2014. Either way, Toronto's fever had broken – the strange mayoralty of Rob Ford was ending.

My smart phone died then, giving me a moment to focus on reading the decision. And the more I read, the more it seemed that this story could not have ended any other way. Like Shakespearean tragedies and Greek myths, the real-life story revolved around a character whose flaws were initially perceived as assets. The same qualities that elevated Ford to power had finally laid him low, and he ended where he began – an outsider shunned in the corridors of power but still beloved by the high school football players he coaches (he would leave a council meeting to coach them to a loss in the provincial championship game the very next day, and advise them, as they teared up, to hold their heads high). Ford's career has been defined by elevating nickel-and-dime items to city-wide prominence – watering plants at city hall, serving dinner during council meetings, rented bunny suits, plastic bags that cost a nickel – so it was particularly fitting that he got removed from office due to a seemingly petty matter: a mere $3,150 in donations to be repaid.

Hackland's ruling laid bare in a few simple words those character traits that have defined Rob Ford's career: the decision noted a 'stubborn sense of entitlement,' a 'dismissive and confrontational attitude' toward procedures and those who enforce them, 'ignorance' and a 'lack of diligence in securing professional advice amounting to wilful blindness.'

Those qualities are precisely what made him appear to be a scrappy and authentic outsider to voters who thought he might be what the city needed in 2010. They led him to early victories as he steamrolled council and Queen's Park in early 2011. But it was those same qualities that inspired a citizen uprising over the budget, transit and the waterfront, that led city council to start routinely overruling him and, finally, that gave a judge no legal choice but to remove him from office. He erected a pigheaded barricade with stubborn, prideful ignorance, and manned that barricade to the very end.

Of course, it was not completely over yet. A stay of the order allowed him to remain on the job pending appeal – until late January at least. That appeal would have to be heard. Legal questions would stretch the last days of Ford's term out for another month or two – or longer. But already, at the council meeting the next day, his most loyal and loudmouthed hench-man, Giorgio Mammoliti, had turned on him again, resigning from the mayor's executive committee and demanding that Ford step aside pending appeal, claiming it was time for the city to get over the partisanship of the Ford era and move on. Denzil Minnan-Wong and Doug Holyday said unflattering things about Ford and hedged on clarifying their continued support of him. Councillor Shelley Carroll talked about running for mayor in a possible by-election, and the press gallery was handicapping the race to come – what were Adam Vaughan's chances? Karen Stintz's? John Tory's? Olivia Chow's? Ford might still rise again, but city hall has already moved on to a new fight – over where it will go next.

Toronto is ready for that discussion. As dominating a presence as Ford has been in the political conversation for two years, his chief legacy has been to paralyze the city. We've spent the time since his election refighting the garbage strike of 2009, reversing some of the new revenue tools of 2007 and revisiting the plastic-bag fee and bike-lane debates of 2010. Surveying the landscape at the end of the Ford administration, we find ourselves in many ways back near where we started: the Vehicle Registration Tax was repealed, the quest for new sources of money back on, the new bike lanes removed, the plastic-bag issue driving everyone nuts. And after all the traumatic hand-wringing, the budget – a draft was released the same week the judge's order was handed down – isn't much closer to (or further away from) being struc-turally balanced than it was the day Ford was elected. We are heading for a fight over laying off police and firefighters and ending automated leaf-gathering in Etobicoke.

There are a few issues Ford supporters will point to as enduring victories: he contracted out garbage collection in part of the city, legislated an end to TTC strikes and negotiated a deal with the city's other unions that would prevent any strikes for four years.

And there are even some moves his detractors would agree were uncontested wins for the city, especially on the hiring of senior bureaucrats. Jennifer Keesmaat is a chief city planner after a downtown elitist's heart, new TTC head Andy Byford is a transit pro by anyone's estimation, and if Gene Jones could lead a turnaround in the public housing agency in Detroit, he seems well-equipped to help move Toronto Community Housing forward. Some wonder if other candidates might have applied for these jobs if we'd had a less controversial mayor, but I haven't heard anyone denying that we landed some solid, world-leading public executives nonetheless.

Still, the issue that best sums up the Ford administration's effect on Toronto is the biggest: the city's transit plan was confirmed in a big signing ceremony with the province two days after the judge handed down his decision, and it was the same transit plan we had when Ford arrived in office, except delayed by about two years – stalled by a bitter fight over the mayor's stubborn indulgence of fantasy and his attempts to exercise power in the service of it.

On the same course as before, but two years behind – a statement that applies to many things about the city after Ford. But there *is* one big difference. We now proceed – however delayed – having gone through a thorough, very public debate about transit planning, a debate in which citizen activists campaigned and a city council emboldened by public support awoke to its own authority. A blue-ribbon panel of experts weighed in, and virtually everyone in the city learned something about how population density and cost can inform a decision about transportation technology. As a direct result of that debate, we have now begun to publicly recognize the need for a downtown-relief subway line that transit wonks have spent decades quietly insisting should be added – and we're trying to figure out how to pay for it.

Of course, Ford didn't lead that public debate about transit (his contribution was limited to repeating a mantra of 'subways, subways, subways'), but he provoked it. Without Ford bringing his outsider grumblers into the conversation, and without the vitriolic opposition he and his supporters inspired, a public debate we dearly needed, one we never had under Miller or Lastman, would never have happened.

There's another way in which the case that threw Ford out of office is a perfect symbolic end to his administration. The court case began when a private citizen named Paul Magder found a pro-bono lawyer and filed a complaint about Ford's behaviour with the courts. A citizen was inspired to activism by the actions of a mayor. And that citizen changed the course of the city. If I were imagining the story, I could not have written a better ending.

IV

INVENTING THE TORONTO
OF TOMORROW

1

Almost every problem that every city faces – crime, poverty, inequality, social dysfunction – is what planners, designers and business experts call a 'wicked' problem. An old-fashioned 'tame' problem is relatively linear. We might have a river we can't cross. How do we solve it? Build a bridge. Make sure it's structurally sound. Problem solved: we can now cross the river.

A wicked problem is complex and difficult to define – it's often, in fact, a symptom or effect of other problems – and it involves multiple stakeholders who cannot agree on what exactly the problem is. And it's equally difficult to define or measure what a successful solution would achieve. According to this thinking, one of the key characteristics of a wicked problem is that it does not have a right or wrong answer, only better or worse answers. And the theory holds that the way to deal with wicked problems is not by engineering a perfectly designed solution, but rather to set up a perfectly designed process that allows all the various constituencies – in government terms, the citizens – to make sense of the problem and find multiple ways to deal with it. The consultant (and wicked problem expert) Jeff Conklin told U of T's *Rotman Magazine* that 'dealing with wicked problems is not at all a matter of coming up with the best answer; rather, it's about engaging stakeholders in a robust and healthy process of making sense of the problem's dimensions.' Without such a process, he said, we get fragmentation, 'a condition in which the stakeholders in a situation see themselves as more separate than united. The fragmented pieces are, in essence, the perspectives, understandings and intentions of the collaborators, all of whom are convinced that their version of the problem is correct ... The antidote to fragmentation is shared understanding and shared commitment.'

The answers, then, are in the process, just as the themes and lessons of any story lie not in its conclusion but in the unfolding of the plot. And, as I've argued throughout this book, the big-picture answers to Toronto's current growing pains – not just for the next mayor and the council he or she leads but for the city as a whole – will be found by turning to those principles that have built Toronto: creating more democracy and infrastructure that harness our diversity and allow it to thrive. In many ways, the success and vibrancy of central Toronto is a function of the gradual, community-level processes that created those neighbourhoods and provided infrastructure that allowed a diverse community to meet its own needs. The problems faced in the less vibrant neighbourhoods of the inner suburbs are a function of a process of central planning that built neighbourhoods according to what some engineer's plan said a community should want and be happy with.

People talk about de-amalgamation of the former municipalities that make up Toronto as a solution. But regional issues such as transit and policing would not be better served through de-amalgamation, and the process involved in untangling the various areas from each other looks a lot like trying to put the toothpaste back into the tube. At this stage, a de-amalgamation prompted by downtown residents' resentment at having Rob Ford foisted on them would amount to little more than the privileged abandoning the poor – a sort of reversal of the 'white flight' that hollowed out and depressed American cities in the 1960s and 1970s. It would also be abandoning some of the diversity in Toronto's population – ethnic, income, lifestyle and otherwise – that has helped make Toronto great. We are in this together, and the solutions to our problems are ones we'll find together.

As much as amalgamation has created an identity crisis, our identity as a diverse global city is contained in the whole of the new Toronto, not in parts of it. So the solution to our conflicts doesn't lie in partitioning off the warring segments. Indeed, on some major infrastructural issues, like transit, it's becoming clear we need more regional coordination across the GTA. That said, a lot could be accomplished by devolving power over neighbourhood issues ever closer to the neighbourhood level. Many of the complaints we see emerging throughout the amalgamated city's history – under all three post-amalgamation mayors – emerge from a sense among the citizenry that their voices and concerns are not heard at city hall. Setting up ways for people to more directly influence government at the ultra-local level is important everywhere, but it is especially key in neighbourhoods like Woburn in Scarborough, which are both physically and demographically distant from the levers of power and those who wield them. When you give people authority over their local environment, they feel a sense of ownership over it, and they can often point to better solutions to their challenges than any outsider could.

The largely ceremonial community councils that today deal with local zoning and speed bumps are made up solely of the local city councillors from the former municipalities the community councils represent. Those councils could be given more authority over local issues, and real power to allocate budgets for development and grants to community groups and agencies, for example. But there are currently only four community councils, and there are 144 distinct neighbourhoods in Toronto. In New York City, there are borough presidents for the large regional areas of the city, as well as fifty-nine different volunteer 'community boards' who advise city council. In London, England, thirty-three elected borough or city councils (many composed of more than fifty councillors) are the primary government service providers and decision-makers.

If we want to engage citizens in Toronto, we could devolve authority even further, beyond the community-council level, and form neighbourhood assemblies that would have actual authority over certain local issues and spending. This is not such a far-fetched idea; after all, we've already done something similar in the small-business sector. In the late 1960s, the strip of Bloor Street West near Swansea and Runnymede, just west of High Park, had become depressed. Big regional shopping malls like Yorkdale and Sherway Gardens had opened, and in 1968 the Bloor-Danforth subway line had extended under the street west to Islington. The construction process killed activity on the Bloor West strip, and the newly opened route didn't help matters, since now people who used to travel through the neighbourhood by streetcar instead travelled past it underground. Local shopkeepers struggled to stay in business.

Some of these shopkeepers got together and cast a cold eye on the very malls that were threatening their livelihoods. They noticed how fees paid to the mall's management funded marketing, common area improvements, festivals and advertising. They drafted a scheme to form a similar model for their neighbourhood, and went to the city for approval. If the majority of business and commercial property owners in the area agreed, they asked, would the city tender an additional levy on their property taxes and return it to the group to spend on marketing and improving the neighbourhood?

The result was the Bloor West Village Business Improvement Area, the first such organization in the world. The scheme successfully revitalized the area's commercial landscape and inspired neighbourhoods across the city to follow suit. Today there are more than seventy BIAS in Toronto, and the concept has been exported to the rest of Canada and around the world. There are over five hundred BIAS in Canada, more than twelve hundred similarly structured groups across the United States and still more in Europe, Australia and Africa. John Kiru, the executive director of the Toronto Association of Business Improvement Areas told me the concept was 'Toronto's best export,' a way of improving and building the city by giving local business owners a small form of local government responsibility, including what is essentially taxing and spending power.

What if a similar model was implemented for neighbourhood residents – with an elected volunteer local neighbourhood council that has a budget for local initiatives and improvements and holds public meetings for issues of local concern? Representatives from those neighbourhood councils could form part of the community council, which reports now to city council, creating an accountable and empowered chain of representation for citizens for neighbourhood, area-wide and regional issues.

But that's just one suggestion, and there are any number of other existing, well-articulated, no-brainer ideas to make the city's government more accessible. A presentation by Dave Meslin that was displayed at city hall in 2012 included a proposal to introduce ranked balloting (which would make elections fairer and more open); implement clearer, corporate-style advertising to announce public meetings and hearings; and hold important meetings at more convenient times (i.e., when people are not at work). Such reforms would have the simultaneous effect of emphasizing 'customer service' and making citizen involvement easier and more attractive. And that is one of the key hurdles to jump in making Toronto's democracy even stronger than it has been. One of the inspiring things about following local politics is seeing how effectively small groups of citizens can make a difference once they know how to navigate the system. But one of the most frustrating things is seeing how difficult it is for most people to figure out how that system works. You can fight city hall, but it involves a steep learning curve; as a result, the people who are most successful in influencing the city are those already most inclined to be involved.

The larger infrastructure projects that require the city's involvement – transit expansion, the official plan, widespread redevelopment such as in Regent Park or the Port Lands – should be subject to widespread community hearings in the neighbourhoods affected and transparent public debate across the city. One of the great weaknesses of Transit City was that it was never subject to open debate and voting at city council, and consequently was poorly understood by the public. On the other hand, the Port Lands redevelopment process had benefitted from years of careful planning and debate and consultation in the area affected; it was a far quicker task therefore to prevent it from being hijacked by the Fords.

Chicago's Ward 49, like some cities in Europe and Latin America, has adopted a system of participatory budgeting that sees the public directly involved in debating and deciding annual spending priorities. The Toronto Community Housing Corporation has introduced a similar process of direct resident involvement in budgeting, and its meetings are packed with people carefully considering alternatives, and standing behind the difficult decisions they have made together. If you give people an opportunity to participate in the process, they seize it.

Specific proposals aside, we need a council-wide recognition that solutions to Toronto's problems are going to spring up from the city's neighbourhoods. Because, as Jane Jacobs reminded Richard Florida, the solutions to problems always lie in the community where the problem exists. And a crowd consensus will almost always produce better answers than even its smartest member will acting alone. While you cannot impose citizen engagement and a sense of community on people, you can build the infrastructure to allow them to form a community and express themselves, and then follow their lead.

2

It's obvious that the next leader of Toronto – or the next group of leaders – will need to find some way to unify the city. It's imperative that we see ourselves, politically, as one entity, a group of people sharing a city, united in the project of making it better for all of us even as we might disagree on how to get there. A cross-partisan coalition of councillors led by Karen Stintz clearly recognized this when they unveiled a surprising, comprehensive, but flawed transit proposal that they called OneCity in the early summer of 2012. OneCity feels like just a footnote now, but its ambition and potential for uniting Toronto in an honest-to-goodness city-building movement – one that had emerged from a city council that suddenly seemed capable of working together – made city hall watchers giddy. But the city couldn't be unified by a $30 billion infrastructure plan pulled out of the box preassembled and presented as a gift to the citizens. While it was temporarily crushing to see it defeated almost as quickly as it was proposed, there was nothing organic about it. It didn't come from the residents, or suit their needs and wants. It's not how Toronto has ever done things.

And yet building or rebuilding infrastructure – transit infrastructure, road infrastructure, social infrastructure such as parks, schools, community centres, affordable family housing and social services – needs to become a top priority. The city's planners have not kept pace with the continent-leading condo construction we've experienced, and even as the city core becomes home to tens of thousands of new residents and a bunch of formerly industrial main streets in North York, Scarborough and Etobicoke are rebuilt as dense high-rise condo neighbourhoods, we are not building the infrastructure to support those neighbourhoods and ensure they are great places to live. Figuring out how to pay for all of this is one challenge, but just acknowledging that the rapidly growing city needs to invest equally rapidly in infrastructure is a necessary first step if we're to avoid a crisis akin to the one faced by R. C. Harris a century ago.

While it's obvious that Toronto needs the provincial and federal governments to help us fund bigger projects like that – if politicians at city hall agree on anything, it's that a national transit strategy and a national affordable housing strategy are desperately needed – we could do a lot to address some of our inner-suburban problems if we start by thinking a bit smaller, a bit more humbly. Even, or especially, when the task is almost impossibly daunting – such as the challenges of the suburban streetscape – focusing on the ultra-local, small-scale and even the ephemeral might lead to more progress more quickly than any decades-long billion-dollar projects we might draw up at city hall.

This crystallized for me when I started thinking about one of Toronto's grandest traditions, the Canadian National Exhibition – an annual monument to the vibrancy of impermanence. Though many of us immediately conjure rickety roller coasters when we picture the fair, the Ex, in fact, used to be a place where visions of the future were unveiled. 'We've lost a bit of it, but if you think of what these great annual fairs were originally, they were really an opportunity for people to see what was new and exciting,' says Ken Greenberg, former director of urban design and architecture for the City of Toronto, and author of *Walking Home: The Life and Lessons of a City Builder*. In the pre-internet age, the CNE was largely a technological and industrial innovation fair – the place where many people caught their first glimpses of televisions, washing machines and automobiles. 'It was a chance to taste, touch and feel all these things,' Greenberg says.

While the exhibits at the CNE are no longer especially forward-looking, the layout of the fair remains so. If tents and trailers lined up in close proximity can turn the vacant parking lots and roadways of Exhibition Place into a bustling streetscape, perhaps something similar is possible in the vast parking lots that dominate the suburbs, or the forsaken courtyards of highrise-tower housing projects. We tend to think of neighbourhood revitalization as a decades-long infrastructure project, but the CNE is revitalized and 'de-vitalized' every year in a matter of days.

Greenberg believes the transitory nature of the Ex may be a big part of the lesson it teaches. 'We're so bound by rules and regulations around making changes in cities,' he says. 'Zoning, official plans, environmental impact studies, environmental assessments – every time you want to change something, it takes years of study. We're incredibly risk-averse; we've basically created these barriers that make it very hard to experiment. But cities are really about experimentation.'

Indeed, though the CNE itself is a centrally controlled and planned environment – the Exhibition Place board approves vendors and manages the layout of the grounds – it has evolved through more than a century of experience and experimentation. It's a 134-year-old testing process; any element added or subtracted will be there only for a matter of weeks, and can easily be ditched the following year.

Greenberg points out that many of the celebrated changes to New York City over the past decade – the large-scale deployment of bike lanes, the pedestrianization of Times Square – have been implemented in a quick, provisional manner. Erect some temporary barriers, paint the pavement, drag out some patio furniture, and see how it works.

It's an approach Greenberg has seen first-hand, turning many downtown-Mississauga parking lots into temporary farmers' markets. 'When people are looking at long-range transformations that can sometimes take decades, you want to show progress and give people a quick taste of what might come,' he says. 'This is a very valuable concept that has much broader applicability than just a fair.'

Local independent musician David Buchbinder of the Juno Award–nominated Flying Bulgar Klezmer Band has been working on a similar premise with his Diasporic Genius project. He and his colleagues envision the creation of permanent '21st Century Village Squares' across Toronto, built and used by local residents for food, craft and other marketplaces, as well as arts and cultural performances. The group has been establishing a pilot project centred on arts events and community storytelling in Thorncliffe Park, a neighbourhood made up of concrete towers surrounded by parking lots and open courtyards. It kicked off with the Festival of Story during a Neighbours Night Out street festival in the summer of 2012. The idea behind Diasporic Genius is to create a village bazaar–style template that can be adjusted according to the desires, needs and cultural interests of different communities. The photos of the pilot project events and the examples of its vision on the Diasporic Genius website look a lot like the CNE, filled with tents, stalls and marching bands amid the crowds.

'The thing about the Ex is that it [shows how quickly change can occur], but does so in a narrow, first-level kind of way,' says Buchbinder. 'It's not embedded in the community. There are a number of ways you can make an incredible transformation in a space overnight. What we're trying to do is make sure they're part of some ongoing development in the community, that they have roots and resonance.'

Roger Keil, director of the City Institute at York University and head of the Global Suburbanisms project that studies how suburban areas are built, used and adapted to new uses, points out that when you join the involvement of local residents to the idea of experimentation, it can help point the way to revitalization that is more community-driven and lasting. In tower neighbour-hoods, for example, 'I'd look one step further and look for more semi-permanence, structures that can be flexible and modular, where the way the space is configured and used can be changed, to allow rapid turnover as neighbourhoods evolve.' Less transitory than a shantytown, he says, and more so than a city.

Imagine the possibilities if such a zest for experimentation took hold in the city. The various perspectives in the transit debate might be informed, for example, by the short-term implementa-tion of bus rapid transit – buses running frequently in dedicated lanes on the road, mimicking the behaviour of an LRT – for a limited period on the planned Sheppard and Finch LRT routes.

A proposal that Greenberg and councillor Kristyn Wong-Tam created for wider sidewalks and more pedestrian activity on Yonge Street was successfully tested during a month-long street festival in September 2012. Cars were restricted to two lanes between Gerrard and Queen (instead of the standard four), and patios, benches and street artists occupied the new, larger pedestrian zone. Such temporary projects, actually executed in the real world, have three virtues, Greenberg says. First, they allow us to study the effects of a change in a way no model can simulate. Second, pilot projects help overcome bureaucratic conservativism. Finally, and perhaps most importantly, it takes possibilities out of the world of artist's mock-ups and city plans, and puts them on the street, where citizens can experience them first-hand.

The CNE is gritty, ramshackle and cacophonous – there are the blinking lights of the Ferris wheel, the wailing sirens, that carny shouting, 'Do you wanna go faster?' and the overwhelming rural stench of the Horse Palace. Although it's a far cry from any beautiful artist's rendering, the CNE is vibrant and fun and its energy is derived from the components it brings together in close proximity, giving people something delightful to participate in. And that's exactly what many of our most interesting neighbourhoods accomplish. No architect could have conceived of Kensington Market on a computer desktop. In neighbourhoods like that, the elements that create urban energy have evolved over generations. The annual transformation of the Ex suggests that with the right attitude toward impermanence and experimentation, we might be able to produce, in a similarly short period of time, that same kind of vibrancy in our desolate paved prairies.

And maybe that would be a more fitting approach for Toronto: instead of a single, unifying grand visionary plan, we could launch a thousand different neighbourhood-level projects (perhaps with funding directly controlled by neighbourhood councils!), each geared to the needs and tastes of the communities they serve. Successes could be shared and adopted by other neighbourhoods, failures would be recognized quickly and wouldn't devour much time or money. Acting separately in different ways, the various parts of Toronto could make themselves stronger and, over time, make each other even stronger.

3

I keep talking about the many processes we might implement to make our democracy work better, even as the democratic process the city faces at the apparent conclusion of the Rob Ford story is a very specific one: selecting a mayor. If Ford loses his appeal and vacates his seat, the task will be at hand just as you read this book. If he somehow wins his appeal, we still face that same decision in an election that will kick off within a year. In either case, the candidates are already sizing up each other and their own chances. Perhaps some of the ways to build communities and community engagement I've been discussing in this chapter will form part of our next leader's platform. But what kind of person should that leader be?

I'm afraid I have no specific endorsement to offer from among the likely (and unlikely) candidates whose names have been tossed around. Ford has emphatically demonstrated he's not up to the job, and that he should be defeated when (or if) he stands for re-election. There are lots of reasons, including late 2012 polls that show him with unfavourable ratings around 60 per cent or higher (even 34 per cent of those who voted for him in 2010 are not planning to vote for him again), to think voters have gotten that message, too. But beyond that, and simply put, the city would be best served by a vigorous election campaign featuring a lot of strong candidates. Such a campaign would give us a chance to see how our next mayor would approach the job and what attitude and ideas the successful candidate would bring to it. And those factors are perhaps more important than the particulars of any candidate's biography.

Obviously, the experience of the Rob Ford clown show has made clear a few traits are desperately needed in our next mayor: someone intelligent and articulate enough to understand policy discussions and meaningfully participate in them; someone composed enough in his or her personal life to avoid providing a constant distraction from city business; someone with the political skills to respectfully, if vigorously, lead a debate among city councillors and find a consensus or make smart compromises to push forward an agenda. And, please, someone who won't try to reverse all the decisions of the recent past and instead will begin talking about how to move forward from where we are.

Ford's supporters – especially his former supporters who lament his personal failings – talk a lot about 'fiscal responsibility,' and clearly a big part of his appeal is the belief that we need to spend within our means. This is a fine message, and as far as cutting perks like staff parties go, it maybe bore emphasizing for symbolic reasons at the very least. But the emphasis on cutting waste and inefficiency is actually shared across the political spectrum. David Miller and Shelley Carroll's final budget in 2010 cut about as much spending by finding efficiencies as Rob Ford and Mike Del Grande's proposed 2013 budget does.

Meanwhile, it's important that the next mayor be aware that fiscal responsibility includes not just parsimony but reality: the need to pay for things, and to raise the revenue to pay for things, is unavoidable. Toronto cannot continue to enjoy a level of services that are the envy of the province while paying tax rates that are among the lowest. There are more ways to raise the money we need than just property taxes. Sales taxes, parking fees, vehicle registration taxes, road tolls and even income taxes are all possibilities that either the city or the province could implement, and all or most are used in other large North American cities. In some cases, such as building regional transit and roads across the GTA, region-wide sources of revenue (such as sales taxes or an income-tax levy) are appropriate – and necessary. Our next mayor cannot claim to be fiscally responsible if he or she is unwilling to face the fiscal responsibilities that come with funding the growth of a booming metropolis.

Joe Pennachetti, the city manager who presided over Ford's scaremongering about the $775 million budget gap in 2011 and who presented the controversial KPMG report, told a University of Toronto audience in May 2012 that while the city is financially very healthy and has an admirably low debt level, there is virtually no more further money that can be cut from the budget without slashing services. He talked about the need for new revenue to fund transit and affordable housing, advocating a sales tax. A close look at the budget leads to this conclusion.

Yet raising taxes or government revenues is always a tough sell, here and everywhere. But making a tough sell is what we need the next mayor to do, on many fronts. Here's the thing, though: salespeople, since I've introduced that metaphor, don't just shy away from the cost of things, they also emphasize the benefits and value the customers get for their dollars. And when it comes to our taxes and what they can and do buy, we need a mayoral candidate who isn't afraid to talk about the ways investments in infrastructure, public services and smart planning will directly benefit residents. When I visited the mayor of Markham, the cost-cutting conservative Frank Scarpitti, in the honest-to-goodness outer-suburban 905, he talked about how the affluent executives who live in Markham scramble to pay premium fares whenever new rapid bus services or express GO train lines are added. He spoke proudly of how he had recently installed the province's largest free public skating rink as part of a new walkable downtown business and residential core he and his council were building around city hall. He bragged of the urbanist infrastructure and cultural amenities he was investing in, because the current residents of Markham, and the residents he hoped to attract as the city grows, recognized the value of those things in making their lives better. It called to mind R. C. Harris's glorification of public-works projects as grand civic monuments. In Toronto, we've recently – and not just since the dawn of Ford – come to talk about public services and infrastructure as necessities grudgingly administered to the poor as cheaply as possible, or worse, as part of the 'gravy train.' It's about time we saw candidates start talking about the things our tax dollars buy us as necessary elements of the good life. Because they are.

Ford sold inner-suburban residents a lot of snake oil, and it would be disastrous for the city if another candidate just rebottled that serum with a fancier label. But that doesn't mean the symptoms those snake-oil customers hoped he could treat aren't real. There are a lot of people in this city, especially in the inner suburbs, who can see that some neighbourhoods are more equal than others when it comes to good public parks and easy access to transit, services, and the vibrant arts and cultural landscape of city life. The principles of urbanism – as laid out by Jane Jacobs but adapted by other thinkers since, and being studied and expanded in a suburban context by such people as Roger Keil – have a lot to offer in addressing those concerns. But those benefits have to be put forward, because they are not always obvious. As the saying goes, if Henry Ford had asked people what they wanted, they would have asked him to design a faster horse. He offered a better solution, a more expensive one in the short term, but one that was transformative in ways his potential customers could not have envisioned.

Good politicians can convince people, rather than just packaging their existing opinions into slogans. We need that kind of politician as mayor, someone to lead public opinion rather than catering to popular, ignorant prejudices. And not just when it comes to the budget and taxes.

Because if the next mayor is going to be successful in curing what ails Toronto, he or she will need to speak to – and for – the city as a whole, rather than lining up on one side of the downtown-suburban divide that has come to define our politics since amalgamation. There, stark differences that exist among Toronto's neighbourhoods right now encourage people to think about how the city serves them differently, and lead them into trumped-up divides: car drivers versus cyclists, and so on. But the way to escape those same old, antagonistic arguments is to recognize the city's diversity, and beat a path forward by encouraging strength in that diversity.

The various areas of the city can all be made better, and stronger, and the recipe for strength might be different in each place, depending on the situation they're in right now. And so while some things, like mass transit, need to be handled on a city-wide or even region-wide level, the needs of each neighbourhood are not universal, and there's no one-size-fits-all recipe for improving livability. For a mayoral candidate, uniting the city through its diversity doesn't mean finding a way to convince residents in Kensington Market or Woburn or Yonge and Eglinton or Rexdale that they need to sublimate their needs to the greater good; it means talking with residents of each of those neighbourhoods about what specific things will make the city they live in stronger, and making those residents a part of making it happen.

On Jarvis Street, say, residents might say making it safer and easier for them to bike to work is a priority. On Brown's Line, making it easier to bike to reliable transit could be more viable. Meanwhile, in Kingston-Galloway, more frequent and reliable bus service might make the most noticeable transportation difference quickly. In some neighbourhoods, smart mid-rise development could make housing more affordable and create a population density that can make possible a more vibrant retail area. In other neighbourhoods, introducing more commercial and industrial development might do the same thing. And so on. Ultimately, the most livable parts of the city need to become more affordable and the most affordable neighbourhoods more livable.

A lot of people studying the situation in Toronto have called for ways to make the mayor's office stronger – either by granting more power to the office or through the introduction of a formal party system, making city council function more like a parliament where a mayor with a majority government would function the way the prime minister does. I can see the appeal of both of those suggestions – and I can see how, in theory, a more powerful office would likely attract a better calibre of candidate. But I also think those ideas are mistaken. The relative weakness of the mayor, and his or her need to build a majority issue by issue with city councillors from every part of Toronto, is a feature of our system, not a bug. It certainly makes getting things done more difficult, but our system also means that the diversity of the city is expressed in our politics, and that democracy is more than a once-every-four-years thing: it's a constant process played out at every council and committee meeting.

The formally non-partisan alignment of city council is what allows councillors to be responsive to the concerns of their residents; it's what enabled city council to tap into the mood of the residents and overrule Rob Ford on so many occasions. Under the current system, observers – including me – sometimes shorthandedly refer to the left and right of council, and sometimes add a third category, the centre (or 'mushy middle'). But this ignores that council is formally forty-five separate independent elected officials, and that even in that number there are actually five or six or more voting blocs constantly negotiating with each other.

I hope that council, for the rest of this term and beyond, remains aware of the power it has, collectively – a power that it demonstrated in standing up to Rob Ford. In a city as diverse as Toronto, and given our proud history of resisting the whims of powerful elites, it's entirely appropriate that at city hall, final authority rests in the quarrelling, often chaotic, collective – not in the hands of any one person or office.

But that means, too, that our next mayor must win the confidence, from the beginning and at every stage thereafter, of the councillors who represent the varied and far-flung neighbourhoods of the city. There are many ways to build a working consensus among an ego-driven group like Toronto city council – persuasion, compromise and old-fashioned horse-trading among them – but those routes all lead to the ability to govern, while the alternative leads to frustration. I'd note, though, that the most effective tool is popularity: if a councillor believes the mayor has the support of his or her local constituents, the mayor will almost always have the support of that councillor.

And so whoever wants to lead the city next will need to be able to communicate with the residents of the various areas of the city – communication works two ways, and it is equally important in both. The next mayor will have to listen to and understand the concerns and priorities of residents from across the entire city, downtown and suburbs, north and south, east and west, and give voice to those concerns and priorities in ways that help people elsewhere in the city understand and appreciate them. And the next mayor must also be able to inspire and persuade voters from every corner of the city with a vision of the next stage of the city's growth with benefit to all of us, together.

All of that, I'm sure, sounds like a wish list – and it is. But these are the qualities the city needs now in a mayor, and if we get someone with at least a handful of these abilities, I think they can both win an election and lead the city into a better future. Of course, it's possible that someone – possibly even Rob Ford – will instead win by cynically pitting one part of the city against another again, playing down our real needs and playing up our differences, trying to turn Toronto's diversity into a weakness. I hope we've moved past that, and the city's history makes me confident we have. But after the last several years, very little in Toronto politics could surprise me. Even in the event that we do reward another divider, though, the city's history also makes me confident that our strong city council and capacity for citizen activism will again limit the damage, and eventually turn us toward progress.

4

Here's the great idea on which Toronto is built: diversity. At a time when cities have become the economic and cultural engines of the world, and while Toronto has emerged as a global city, the idea that has served as its organizing principle has been revealed as one of the key organizing principles of any society or organization. It's not just an organizing principle for cities and neighbourhoods, it's how ecosystems thrive, it's how the free market works, it's the quality that makes the internet the most valuable information resource in history. Provided that there's infrastructure in place to allow the many different pieces to interact, and a democratic structure in place to allow everyone to participate, then diversity is one of the keys to any successful system.

But diversity is messy. In a natural ecosystem, animals feed off one another; in the marketplace, businesses fail and whole industries become obsolete, bankrupting shareholders and throwing employees out of work; on the internet, bitter arguments dominate comment sections on every website that still possesses them. And in cities, different populations and ideas and lifestyles intersect and sometimes collide. Throughout our history, that process has always been filled with conflict, as angry and ugly as it is fascinating. And there's no reason to expect the present and future to be any different – democracy and diversity work through friction. But the heat generated by all that friction can produce light to illuminate the path forward and energy to propel us along that path.

Diversity is the source of our strength but it has also, since amalgamation, been increasingly the source of our struggles. In some ways, a lack of diversity has led to new challenges. A sorting of the population by wealth, ethnicity and immigration status has led to a situation where differing perspectives and lifestyles are isolated from each other, where the upwardly mobile and those who continue to struggle live in vastly different Torontos.

And yet through its history, Toronto has been self-correcting through democracy, and our politics – as crazy and dysfunctional as it often is – continues to provide a crude mechanism for illuminating the problems we need to address. In the post-amalgamation era, Mel Lastman represented the old Metro establishment, who thought that the wealthy and powerful could iron out the city's wrinkles themselves. David Miller's long-shot victory represented an uprising of the new emerging establishment, the headstrong, upwardly mobile citizens who define the creative class, those who are confidently fluent in urbanism and demand that the government accommodate them. Rob Ford's surprising election, in turn, represented a cry from those who belonged to neither of those elite groups, and whose first-hand observation of the devolution of their own neighbourhoods made them suspicious of burdensome schemes imposed by politicians they didn't feel represented them.

And throughout the process, between these huge course-changing elections, city council itself has kept the extremes of all sides in check. Council uncovered the scandal of the MFP under Lastman even as councillors like Jack Layton made progress toward housing the homeless and installing bike infrastructure. Miller's careful attempts to build and maintain council consensus and to pay close attention to the needs of suburban areas outside his base moderated the pace of urbanization (enraging some of his allies). When Ford's extreme dislike and distrust for all but the most basic of government operations showed itself to be more (and less) than voters thought they were asking for, city council responded to those voters by assuming leadership of the city themselves. Democracy has continued to ensure that the diversity of the broader city expresses itself, sometimes clumsily, to keep the city moving forward, even if on an erratic, zig-zag course.

And under Lastman, Miller and Ford, the city as a whole has continued to grow and succeed. The city is bigger than its mayor, and the city is bigger than its government. Indeed, the ways that much of the city thrived before and during the governments of Lastman, Miller and Ford raise the question of how important a mayor really is. It's not that nothing changed under those different mayors. And the substantial changes each made will likely, in the long term, alter the course of the city. It's just that for as much as these mayors have pursued radically different policies from one another, the city's trajectory is only ever altered a few degrees by any given mayor's term in office. And city council and the population at large serve to tweak even those incremental changes in direction. The mayor is a symbolically important figure, and can serve as the leader of the council and the city, but the mayor is not a dictator. That's our system working as it should.

And now it's interesting to observe that after Lastman, Miller and Ford have each risen and fallen, one of their primary roles seems to have been bringing their differing constituencies – and their most vocal opponents – into the civic conversation. Even if that engagement often looks like little more than a shouting match, the priorities and needs of all those parts of the Toronto electorate are now a regular part of the political story we tell ourselves. One of the key things a mayor can do, especially in our weak-mayor system, is serve as the focal point of the debate the city's citizens have with themselves about where they are going together.

As this book is published, our crazy politics have just gotten crazier – Rob Ford ordered out of office by a judge, and city council scrambling to figure out what happens next: appoint an interim mayor? Hold a by-election? Who will run? Will the decision be overturned on appeal? Suddenly, everything is uncertain. Yet even in that uncertainty, Toronto is now in an excellent position to have a real debate about its future – and an emergency decision about who should be mayor, in the wake of all the battles we've recently gone through, provides as big a spotlight for that debate as we're ever likely to see. Whatever the result, that spotlight is likely to continue shining, and the debate to continue unfolding, at least until 2014, when the regularly scheduled election will allow for an opportunity to affirm or revise whatever decisions we make today – and at that point I expect every ward-level city-council race will be somehow a part of that debate, since circumstances have conspired to make every councillor a player in the unfolding drama. There is no script for the situation we're in at the dawn of 2013, no default options to choose: we have to improvise.

People always want to weigh in on whether Lastman and Miller and Ford are 'good' or 'bad' mayors. But the question is beside the point – all of them have been *necessary* mayors. All gave their supporters' ideas and concerns a push forward, and all provoked their opponents to mobilize. Today, public passion about city politics is higher than it ever has been in my lifetime. The problems and opportunities the city is facing have crystallized. The messy events of the past two years – indeed, of the past decade and a half – have provided a moment of unusual clarity for Toronto.

That's partly what Toronto's history teaches us about how diversity works in a democracy: forces of action and reaction engage in direct conflict. Mackenzie fought for democracy in reaction to a corrupt colonial system; R. C. Harris built infrastructure in reaction to a level of neglect that had become a crisis; Jane Jacobs helped the city realize its neighbourhood strengths in reaction to the impending bulldozing of many of those strengths. The effects of all these movements were felt for generations, defining the affirmative principles that helped build one of the most livable cities in the world.

And it is how the current generation of Torontonians, gripped by an identity crisis since amalgamation created a new, sprawling city made up of different kinds of places built at different times and encouraging different ways of living – a more diverse Toronto than has ever existed before, and suddenly in a political crisis created by one of the strangest mayoral stories we've ever lived through – will find a way forward. We need to build a larger infrastructure. Foster a more powerful democracy. Harness the unrivalled strength of our city's diversity. And in the aftermath of a generation of bitter political conflicts, write a new mythology for the new city together, and invent Toronto once again.

ACKNOWLEDGMENTS

Much of the material in this book originally appeared – sometimes in substantially different form, sometimes almost identically – in *The Grid* and its predecessor, *Eye Weekly*, as well as *Spacing* magazine, *Yonge Street*, *Canadian Immigrant* and the Coach House Books collection *uTOpia: Towards a New Toronto*. Those publications gave me the time, the money, the freedom and the excuse to find and tell these stories, and for that I am thankful to all the editors and publishers I have worked with along the way.

I have benefitted much from the reporting and thinking of other writers, and this book is particularly informed by the writing and reporting of some contemporary Toronto journalists.

John Lorinc, whose book *The New City* is wonderful, and whose reporting on Toronto is consistently insightful, was particularly helpful. His writing about the life of R. C. Harris in the *Globe and Mail*, and particularly in an article entitled 'The City Builder' that appeared in *Spacing* magazine in Winter 2006 and on his Harris-themed blog The R.C. Harris Project (www.thercharrisproject.blogspot.com), as well as a conversation with him, form a crutch that holds up most of the section about Harris.

I owe my understanding of William Lyon Mackenzie to a much broader range of sources, but I found former Toronto mayor John Sewell's 2002 biography *Mackenzie* particularly helpful.

Among many histories of the fight to stop the Spadina Expressway, I owe a particular debt to a memoir of the battle written by Adam Vaughan for *Eye Weekly* in June 2006.

The Toronto writer who may be the heir to Jane Jacobs's influence on world thinking about cities is Doug Saunders, whose *Arrival City* tackles the problems of inner suburban immigration hubs around the world head on. My quote from Saunders comparing London to Toronto comes from an interview he gave to *Toronto Life* in 2010, and a piece he wrote for that magazine in 2006 entitled 'You Are Here' offers a great primer on how the central city evolved (and the quote about the city having 'no symbolic heart' found on page 37.)

The work of the reporters of the Toronto City Hall press gallery, past and present, is consistently excellent, and without their efforts

I could not do the job I do every week as an analyst in *The Grid* nor could I have written this book – especially (but not only) Jeff Gray, John Barber, Jennifer Lewington and Kelly Grant of the *Globe and Mail*; Daniel Dale, Donovan Vincent, Robyn Doolittle, David Rider and Royson James of the *Toronto Star*; Don Peat and (at one time) Rob Granatstein of the *Toronto Sun*; David Nickle of *Toronto Community News*; Philip Preville of *Toronto Life*; Hamutal Dotan of *Torontoist*; John McGrath of *OpenFile*; Matt Elliott of *Metro*; and my *Eye Weekly/The Grid* colleagues Chris Bilton, who acted as my eyes and ears on the 2010 campaign trail while I was stuck in the office editing, and Dale Duncan, who reported from City Hall for us for a few years and shared her findings and insights with me every day. I learned of Vive Nano's India strategy from a report in *Yonge Street* by Piali Roy. My understanding about how the citizen-led political reaction to Doug Ford's Waterfront proposal formed and mobilized is informed by the reporting of independent journalist David Hains. If you're looking for a history of Scarborough, and how it evolved, the book to get is *A History of Scarborough*, edited by Robert R. Bonis – I sincerely hope you still can get it at public libraries in Scarborough.

The Coach House *uTOpia* series offers a great summary of the Miller years in office, and I drew on a couple essays in its final installment, *Local Motion*, in particular in writing this book: Catherine Porter's 'The Boxer' for information about Jutta Mason's work in Dufferin Grove Park, Kelly Grant's 'The Budget and You' for an introduction to participatory budgeting, and Denise Balkissoon's 'About Face' for information about the evolution of patios in Toronto.

In more general terms, my thinking about Toronto has been influenced by, among many, many others, Amy Lavender Harris's *Imagining Toronto*, Robert Fulford's *Accidental City*, Christopher Kennedy's *The Evolution of Great World Cities*, Shawn Micallef's *Stroll* and John Bentley Mays's *Emerald City*. And like everyone else, by Jane Jacobs. But you knew that already.

ABOUT THE AUTHOR

Edward Keenan has been writing about Toronto's politics and culture for over ten years, most recently as a Senior Editor at *The Grid* and a columnist at *Spacing* magazine. He is a nine-time National Magazine Award finalist, and was shortlisted for best blogger at the 2012 Canadian Online Publishing Awards. He serves on the faculty of the Academy of the Impossible and coaches a children's hockey team. He lives in the Junction with his wife, Rebecca, and their three children. You can find him on Twitter @thekeenanwire.

Typeset in Goluska and Figgins Sans.
Goluska was designed by Canadian type designer Rod McDonald to honour his long-time friend Glenn Goluska, 1947–2011.
Goluska was one of Canada's finest designers, who, while working
at Coach House in the 1970s, fell in love with Linotype and the
work of the noted American typographer and type designer
William Addison Dwiggins. The typeface Goluska is a homage to
Dwiggins's famous typeface, Electra. Although McDonald tried to
capture some of the feel of Electra, he avoided making a slavish
copy; Goluska is sturdier and the x-height is larger than Electra.
Figgins Sans is Canadian Nick Shinn's OpenType revival of
Vincent Figgins's 1836 design for the Caslon type foundry.

Printed at the old Coach House on bpNichol Lane in Toronto,
Ontario, on Zephyr Antique Laid paper, which was manufactured,
acid-free, in Saint-Jérôme, Quebec, from second-growth forests.
This book was printed with vegetable-based ink on a 1965 Heidel-
berg KORD offset litho press. Its pages were folded on a Baum-
folder, gathered by hand, bound on a Sulby Auto-Minabinda and
trimmed on a Polar single-knife cutter.

Edited for the press by Jason McBride
Designed by Alana Wilcox

Coach House Books
80 bpNichol Lane
Toronto ON M5S 3J4
Canada

416 979 2217
800 367 6360

mail@chbooks.com
www.chbooks.com